More Praise for *Enough Is Enough!*

"In this day and age when endurance is tolerated and even extolled, our society needs to return to some basic values—living in our truth, being one. Jane Straus's *Enough Is Enough!* needs to be read by every man and woman who wants to find a life of authenticity and inspiration. This book will immediately turn you in that direction."
—Daniel Jay Sonkin, Ph.D., psychotherapist;
author, *Wounded Boys/Heroic Men*

"Truly an inspirational book. The author speaks from the heart in a clear, articulate way, weaving examples from clients in many diverse circumstances to bring the reader a message about paying attention to our deepest truth and its healing power. This sounds deceptively simple, but the author aptly describes the psychological and bodily distortions that we humans can go through when in fear and provides a path to connect with the extraordinary within each of us."
—Mindy S. Rosenberg, psychologist;
coauthor, *Children and Interparental Violence*

"Jane Straus tackles a complex human dynamic with simplicity and clarity. This book has lessons that most of us need to learn."
—The Reverend Dr. Kikanza Nuri Robins,
Presbyterian pastor; author, *Unspoken Visions*

Enough Is Enough!

Stop Enduring and Start Living Your Extraordinary Life

Jane Straus

Foreword by Carol Adrienne

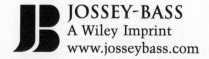

JOSSEY-BASS
A Wiley Imprint
www.josseybass.com

Published by Jossey-Bass
A Wiley Imprint
989 Market Street, San Francisco, CA 94103-1741   www.josseybass.com

Jossey-Bass books and products are available through most bookstores. To contact Jossey-Bass directly call our Customer Care Department within the U.S. at 800-956-7739, outside the U.S. at 317-572-3986, or fax 317-572-4002.

Jossey-Bass also publishes its books in a variety of electronic formats. Some content that appears in print may not be available in electronic books.

Cover and title page art ©Bruno Budrovic/Images.com.

Library of Congress Cataloging-in-Publication Data

Straus, Jane.
Enough is enough!: stop enduring and start living your
extraordinary life / Jane Straus; foreword by Carol Adrienne.
        p. cm.
    ISBN-13: 978-0-7879-7988-1 (alk. paper)
    ISBN-10: 0-7879-7988-0 (alk. paper)
    1. Christian life. I. Title.
    BV4501.3.S775 2005
    248.4—dc22   2005011077

Printed in the United States of America
FIRST EDITION
HB Printing   10 9 8 7 6 5 4 3 2 1

Contents

Foreword   vii
     Carol Adrienne

Preface   ix

Getting Past Groundhog Day: An Introduction   xi

A Word About the Exercises   xix

1.   Enough Is Enough! Begin to End Endurance   1

2.   Exit the Courtroom, Enter the Classroom:
     Let Go of Self-Judgments   17

3.   Remove Your Blinders: See Without Limiting Beliefs   39

4.   Drop Your Acts: Become Who You Already Are   53

5.   Break the Spell of Fear: Make Fear Your Ally   67

6.   Unchain Your Heart: Free Your Feelings   87

7.   Take Off Your Armor: Heal Your Anger
     and Resentment   107

8.   Give Yourself the Gift of Forgiveness: Live
     Compassionately   125

9.   Be Inspired: Knowing, Speaking, and
     Living Your Truth   139

10.   Breaking Free: Create Your Extraordinary Life   151

Acknowledgments   163

About the Author   165

*To those with the courage to keep
an open heart and mind for the sake
of becoming extraordinarily wise,
compassionate, loving, and joyful*

Foreword

If you are ready to change your life, to discover your life purpose, to hear and live your inner truth, then reading Jane Straus's *Enough Is Enough!* will be like opening up the very best birthday present you could ever hope to receive: a gift that includes freedom, relief, joy, and inspired direction. Her book will show you how to take the lid off your life and free yourself from the inner restrictions that have kept you and your life purpose under wraps.

Perhaps the most prevalent question I hear from my readers and clients, no matter how it is phrased—"How do I know when it's time to quit my boring job, change my business, leave my bad marriage . . . ?"—can be simply stated: *How do I know when enough is enough?* The answer, as you will discover in the timely and remarkable book you hold in your hands right now, is to learn to hear the voice of your inner truth and act in alignment with it.

Sometimes I ask participants in my life purpose workshops, If God appeared in this room today and told you what your purpose is, what fears would this bring up? The responses typically include the following: "I might not know how to do it." "I might get it wrong." "I might do it and then find out that wasn't really it." "I might not like it." "I might have to give up certain people and relationships in my life." "I wouldn't know where to start." "I might not have the courage to do what it takes."

I have come to believe that each of us *is* born to create, express, or experience certain things—although our purpose is never limited to just finding the right job title. Oddly, though, I have noticed that the *search* for life purpose sometimes has a darker side, the side that keeps us—as Jane Straus terms it in this book—in the *enduring* mode: putting off living our *real* life until we can put a name to our life purpose. I think a lot of us secretly have this thought: *Tell me what to do (what my purpose is). I'll go do it, and then I'll be happy.* But waiting for some kind of step-by-step, guaranteed plan too often means that we take no small, exploratory steps that *could get the ball rolling!* Instead, we endure our current situation, no matter how difficult it is, until we can be certain everything will "work out" in the future.

We all have our own reasons for staying stuck. But, as this book shows, fear is the underlying culprit, and, most important, there is a way through the fear, out of endurance, and into the arena of the extraordinary. There are no guarantees on the future. Waiting for the infallible green light of a perfect plan can be the rationale for doing nothing at all. Whatever your mode of staying in endurance—gathering more and more data, living in confusion, becoming mired in family responsibilities, or becoming lost in busyness or addiction—the time to live more fully is now.

It does take commitment to have a life worth living. Take a moment right here on the threshold and imagine yourself six months from now or two years from now. Look back at this moment and let out a big sigh of relief—relief that, through grace and belief in yourself, you have been able to *move on*. You have been able to find purpose (maybe not *the* purpose) and meaning in everyday life, and by following the positive signals in your life, you are living the life you were born to live. The fact that you were attracted to this book, and that you hold it in your hands right now, means that you are ready to receive the gifts within the pages of *Enough Is Enough!*—ready to break free of your endurance and start living your extraordinary life now.

El Cerrito, California   Carol Adrienne
July 2005   author, *The Purpose of Your Life*

Preface

Recently, someone asked me when I started writing this book. I didn't mean to be coy as I answered that I didn't start writing *this* book. The book I began writing six years ago was going to be about the value of knowing, speaking, and living our spirit's deepest truths because I believed—and still believe—that if we do not live in alignment with our truth, we inevitably suffer unnecessarily.

It was a topic I thought I knew well. After all, for more than twenty years I had been a successful life coach and personal growth seminar leader. I wrote several drafts of the book, but I just couldn't seem to get it right. Then, quite suddenly, I discovered that I had a brain tumor. Having the tumor removed did wonders for clearing my head! I reflected upon my own life: Was I thriving fully? Was I living what I would define as an extraordinary life? Was I living in alignment with my own truth? I was startled to discover that I could not answer these questions with an unqualified *Yes!* Why not?

As I looked over the preliminary drafts, a question arose that I had never considered: What *stops* us from knowing, speaking, and living our truth and feeling inspired, all or at least most of the time? As I began to explore this question in depth, the answer eventually crystallized into one word: *endurance*. Endurance sneaks up on us as a lack of spark or a nagging dissatisfaction. It is caused by ignoring our deepest longings and aspirations out of the fear that we will fail or be rejected, or because we believe we don't matter enough to pay attention to ourselves.

Oh no. Along with so many people I knew, I had become a card-carrying member of the Endurers Club. To belong, you need only feel somewhat restless, dissatisfied, bored, resentful, overwhelmed, anxious, or hopeless. Having a compulsion or at least one addiction qualifies you too. You can also join if you have mastered telling yourself that you don't deserve better, that this is just the way life is (at least for you), or that it is your fault if you are dissatisfied. If you ever judge yourself harshly, you are automatically elected to the club's steering committee. The not-so-secret password phrase to gain entry to this club is, "Is that all there is?" and its mantra is "Why me?" This was not a club I wanted to belong to anymore! Just learning its name was one of the keys to breaking free.

We may learn early on that we're expected to "be strong" and endure pain or discomfort, or always put others' needs ahead of our own; that questioning our negative beliefs, stepping outside the box, even thriving is risky business. Over the years, we come to believe that being vulnerable is dangerous; we could get hurt, humiliated, or even rejected. If we fall under the spell of these fears, we lose touch with our spirit's longings and deepest truths. Then we honestly wonder if that really *is* all there is to life.

Once I understood the connection between fear and endurance, I knew why I hadn't been living as fully and vibrantly as I could be. Over the past few years, I have shared these ideas with my clients. I watch the proverbial light bulb go on whenever I mention the word "endurance." We all seem to get it intuitively: either we are thriving or we are enduring. We are either free or prisoners of our fears, self-judgments, and old beliefs about how things have to be. It's that clear. Endurance is a prison. Yet each of us already has the key in our pocket. We can take it out and unlock the door.

I wrote this book, in the end, because I couldn't *not* write this book. In the end, it turned out to be about truth, because when we stop enduring and break the spell of fear that has held us hostage, we hear our own clear voice of truth beckoning us to create and revel in our unique and extraordinary life.

I look forward to your joining me on this remarkable journey.

Northern California   Jane Straus
July 2005

Getting Past Groundhog Day:
An Introduction

> The greatest gift we can give to anybody is the gift
> of our honest self.
>
> —*Fred Rogers*

Have you seen the movie *Groundhog Day?* Bill Murray plays Phil, a cynical weatherman who wakes up every morning to the same miserable day over and over again, and there doesn't seem to be anything he can do to change the situation.

As the movie starts, Phil finds himself in Punxsutawney, Pennsylvania, covering the annual Groundhog Day festivities for the fourth year in a row. He doesn't try to hide his frustration at being stuck with this silly assignment again. When the clock-radio wakes him up with a Sonny and Cher tune followed by the announcement that it's Groundhog Day, he gets up and goes to work—irritated, bored, barely going through the motions of covering the event, and ready to turn around and drive home. This year Phil is there with Rita, his new, kind-hearted producer, and although Phil is attracted to her she considers him callous and distrusts him. After a snowstorm forces them to spend another night in what Phil thinks of as small-town hell, he wakes up the next morning to the clock-radio once again playing the same Sonny and Cher song and announcing Groundhog Day. Something very strange is happening: it's exactly the same day as the day before, but he's the only one who seems to know it.

Because Phil knows exactly what will happen at each moment of the "new" day, he derives some humor out of the situation. But then it happens again: He wakes up the next morning to the same tune.

Again. And again. To avoid boredom, he begins playing pranks on the townspeople, knowing they'll never remember. Day after day, he finds new, creative ways to kill time, including endless, futile strategies to trick Rita into wanting to have sex with him. Eventually, he becomes so bored with the monotony and predictability of his life that he tries to commit suicide. Each day he wakes up with a new plan to do himself in, only to wake up once more to the same tune and the same day.

Finally, Phil tires of his own annoying cynicism. He learns to play the piano, becomes a doctor, gets acquainted with all the townspeople, and each day discovers more to appreciate in Rita. He stops trying to manipulate her by posing as the man he thinks she would want and focuses on becoming the person he wants to be. Finally he awakens to the truth that offering his most vulnerable self to Rita and everyone else is the greatest gift he can offer anyone, including himself.

His reward? The next morning he awakens to a new day . . . with Rita by his side.

Why did Phil keep reliving the same tedious day for such a long time? Why did it take him so long to decide that enough was enough? Why do any of us feel we have no choice but to keep living in frustration, boredom, anger, or hopelessness? What does it take for us to wake up to a brand-new day?

My Wake-Up Call

My own wake-up call came on January 27, 2003—Superbowl Sunday. My husband and I were finally getting an opportunity to put away our pots and pans after a kitchen remodel. Suddenly, I felt crummy. I had a splitting headache, and my heart was pounding for no apparent reason. I announced, as nonchalantly as I could, that I was driving myself to the hospital because, as long as the game was on, there would likely be few people in the emergency room. My husband, of course, was shocked and asked me what the matter was. He would have insisted on driving me, but our young daughter was sick with the flu and couldn't be dragged along, so I made the fifteen-minute drive by myself.

My mother was just recovering from a heart attack, so I thought maybe something was wrong with my heart too, or that I was at the very least having one heck of an anxiety attack. But why would putting pots and pans away trigger anxiety? Fortunately, when I arrived at the emergency room, the place was as quiet as I had hoped. The Superbowl game was not yet at halftime, so no broken heads from drunken brawls or drunk-driving emergencies were yet making their way to the ER.

As soon as I said the words "possible heart problems or anxiety" to the triage nurse, she hooked me up to a heart monitor and stuck a needle in my arm for blood work. I thought, *Wow, this is great care for someone having an anxiety attack.* While the nurses waited for the test results, they asked me all the right questions. No, I had never been treated for anxiety before. No, I personally had no history of heart problems. No, I hadn't been to the emergency room, except once for a back injury.

When the doctor came in and asked how I was feeling, I mentioned that, other than a blasting headache and anxiety, I was just fine. Although he hadn't the slightest bit of bedside manner, he did pay attention. "On a scale of one to ten, how bad is the headache?"

"Oh, maybe an eight." He asked what I had taken, gave me more Tylenol, and waited twenty minutes. "Any better?"

"No, and by the way, how's my heart?"

"Your heart seems fine. Maybe we're barking up the wrong tree. I'd like to do a CT scan."

"On what part of me?"

"Your head."

To placate him and maybe get out of there with some anti-anxiety medication, I agreed. Ten minutes later, he came back looking very concerned. I didn't like that look. "You have a brain tumor. It's a meningioma."

If I didn't have anxiety *before* I entered the ER, I now had a full-blown panic attack. "A what? What is that?" It turns out he didn't really know; he was just reading the radiologist's report. One of the nurses came in with a medical dictionary and read me the definition of *meningioma*. No brain tumor is good, but of all the ones to get, this is the one you are considered "lucky" to have because it is usually not malignant. Lucky me.

Six weeks later, I underwent seven-and-a-half hours of surgery, which was more grueling for my family in the waiting room than it was for me, since I was under anesthesia. My experience was that the tumor was inside me one moment and out the next. But in the weeks before I went under the knife, like most people facing life-threatening circumstances I did an inventory. I knew there was a chance I would die on the table, or wake up and not know life as I had known it for forty-eight years. So this was an auspicious moment to check in with myself. Did I have any regrets? Anything left incomplete?

Why, yes, indeed! There was one big item on my list, something I had been working on in fits and starts for years but could not seem to find enough time to complete, something I had avoided finishing because it was daunting and held the potential to fail. The big-ticket item was this book.

I made it through the surgery just fine, but now there was a new promise to keep. Before the surgery, I said to myself, *If I'm able to think coherently after the tumor is removed, I will write that book. No more excuses.* After all, if I use excuses for not committing to my own goals and dreams, how can I work with others' excuses in coaching sessions?

For many years, I have had a successful life-coaching practice based on helping my clients identify where they are stuck and then start living their own extraordinary lives. If you had asked me before my surgery if I myself were a role model of my own teachings, I would have answered, "Yes, of course . . . well, most of the time." Except I had one little problem: as committed as I was to everyone else around me thriving and not just surviving, I wasn't feeling as passionate about my own life as I knew was possible. It wasn't my family or my work that was the problem. However, faced with possible imminent death, I realized that I must be lying to myself in some way. I was discussing with others the value of 100 percent commitment, and here I was avoiding the one commitment that I knew would make me feel more enthusiastic. Why had I not fully committed to myself?

I started taking some "time in" with myself, reflecting on how I organized my time and paying attention to the methods I used to distract myself from writing. It was easy to sabotage myself, really, and didn't require much creativity because my strategies were well honed and habitual. They all revolved around busyness. I would see too many clients in a day. I would volunteer at my daughter's school because the school needed (and deserved) volunteers in these hard economic times. I would read books to help inspire me to write. I cleaned house a lot, read and wrote too many e-mails, and kept a rigorous focus on minutiae. Who had time to write?

I also complained about all of this. Woe is me; why did I have to work so hard? Why didn't others help me more? Why didn't other parents volunteer more at school? Why didn't I start writing the book years ago, before I had a child? Why is there a universal law of entropy that says that everything (in my house and yours) must go from an orderly state to one of disorder? Clearly, the universe was working against me.

Or was it? Who was the real enemy here?

Finally, I realized that my greatest enemy was not entropy, or a tough economy, or lack of money; my greatest enemy was inside my own head, and it wasn't the tumor. *It was my thoughts.* My fearful thoughts—*I'll never be able to do this, It's too late for me, I can't do this alone*—stopped me from choosing a more extraordinary life for myself, just as fearful thoughts can stop all of us. Somewhere along the way, I chose to ignore something that really mattered to *me*, to my spirit. Afraid of failure, I instead used others' needs as an excuse not to focus on one of my own deepest longings. I disguised my fears by telling myself that I needed to be so dedicated to everyone and everything else that I simply couldn't write. To use the term I discuss with my clients, I found that I was *enduring* in an area of my life where I could instead be feeling excited and challenged.

Endurance: The Double-Edged Sword

Many times we hear people use the word *endurance* in an admiring way to mean prevailing against difficult odds or demonstrating tenacity when faced with a tough challenge, as in an athletic competition, getting a college degree, or in a career. This is what I call perseverance, not endurance. *Endurance* means that we have made a virtue out of staying the course even though a nagging voice keeps whispering that this course is wrong for us or is actually destructive to our best interests. Used in this sense—which is how we use it in this book—endurance describes feeling devoid of inspiration; living a life that feels routine, habitual, or dissatisfying. I was a good example. Although my life was filled with love, family, and friendship, it lacked sufficient spark. Mine was a comfortable sort of endurance, but one that gnawed slowly at my spirit. I was very busy creating a veneer of altruism and satisfaction, but underneath this thin veneer I was afraid of something I was not yet facing.

Successful removal of the brain tumor left me feeling grateful and determined. I made an agreement with my spirit to carve out time for researching and writing this book. I knew that to feel my life was extraordinary by my own definition, I needed to make this book one of my highest obligations to myself. Maybe I'm a particularly difficult case—after all, it took a brain tumor to bring me to my senses! But a wake-up call doesn't have to be so dramatic. For many people, it takes only some quiet reflection to realize it's time to live life differently.

Your Wake-Up Call

We come to counseling, read self-help books, or pursue a spiritual journey for any number of personal reasons. But behind them all is the same feeling of urgency: we sense that our lives, like Phil's in *Groundhog Day*, seem patterned in some way that is uncomfortably predictable yet outside our control. We are confused about who or what is pulling the strings. Is it God, the Universe, our unconscious, karma? No one wants to live like this, yet most of us don't know how we got here or if there is a way to get out. So we continue to *endure*— whether it be emotionally, financially, or spiritually—in the sense that we give in to hardship (from the Latin *durus*, meaning hard) *without questioning the value or necessity of our suffering.*

- Pauline, a single mother, feels that *she must* continue working long hours and leave her two young sons in day care so that she will be able to afford to offer them "the best" in life. She's tired from the commute, feels deprived of quality time with her children, and is bored with her tedious routine. But what else can she do?

- Jim finds himself sitting in front of the TV again, watching sports—just like last night, and the night before, and the night before that. Maybe he shouldn't have gotten that satellite dish. There are just too many games to watch. He reminisces about his days as the high school quarterback and wishes he were in better physical shape. But at the age of forty, he thinks it's too late for that now.

- Fran can't find the Post-it note she wrote to remind herself about a meeting. It must be stuck to one of the other Post-it notes she wrote about other meetings and appointments. She wishes she didn't have quite so many errands and responsibilities, but she knows that if she can just clear a few items off her schedule things will look up. She vows to complete her to-do list soon so she can have time to start that yoga class—the one listed on another Post-it note she can't seem to find.

Do these stories resonate? As with Phil the weatherman, the more attached we become to our habits of endurance (workaholism or any other -ism, too much TV or shopping, virtuous overcommitment to others), the less we are able to imagine other possibilities for ourselves. We remain entrenched in our routine, putting in our time, resigned to enduring as far as we can see into the foreseeable future.

But take heart: you are not doomed to live the same day forever. Think about it. If at least a glimmer of this deeper wisdom—this truth—weren't already alive within us, then we couldn't know (as we watch *Groundhog Day*) not only that it's possible for Phil to resolve his predicament but precisely how he should do it. *But we do know*—long before Phil does—that his fears have kept him enduring and that he needs to pay more attention to what he truly values. It's the same for all of us.

The way out of endurance is through the wake-up call of one's own spirit. If you are questioning whether or not your suffering is *really* inevitable, and whether it's true that you just have to put up with it until death do you part, then you are already paying attention to your spirit's truths.

In this book, you will learn about your own personal habits of endurance—how they look and feel, and maybe where they came from. You will also learn to calm the fears that keep you stuck in endurance, and to pay more attention to your deeper truths. In so doing, you will discover that when you focus on being true to yourself, you begin to manifest your extraordinary life.

For any places you endure a "Why this again?" existence, what inspiring realities would you like to create instead? Listen to your spirit. I'm betting it's whispering "Enough is enough" to you right now.

A Word About the Exercises

This book contains many stories about breaking free from endurance. Some are my own stories; others belong to clients, friends, and seminar participants. (I have altered their names and gender, and the details of their stories, to ensure their privacy.) The exercises in this book offer you an opportunity to rethink your own story and envision future chapters that are more interesting. I recommend that you take the time to explore the exercises, as you will find them powerful, revealing, and energizing.

⏱ Time In ⏱

Whenever you see this symbol, I am offering you specific questions designed to help you connect with the ideas we're talking about. I call it Time In because sometimes you may just need to stop moving ahead to the next idea so that you can have an opportunity to take a few moments to breathe and reflect on your own life.

Process for Change

You'll also have the opportunity to go more deeply into the healing and transformative processes in this book. For these Process exercises, it's a good idea to keep a notebook and pen handy so you can record your insights and inspirations.

Enough Is Enough!

Chapter One

Enough Is Enough!

Begin to End Endurance

Something's boring me. I think it's me.
—*Dylan Thomas*

"I'm sorry I haven't had time to call you," Sharon apologized. "I've been volunteering at my kids' schools. With all the cutbacks, they really need help with getting the kids' lunches every day. Then, of course, there's my work at the hospital, which doesn't leave me any time for myself. And last week, Don and I hosted two business dinners for his clients. Then the boys had homework, soccer, and projects. Sunday is church and, well, there goes the week."

There goes a life! If Sharon were truly happy with all her activities, we could admire her generosity, community spirit, and values. But here is Sharon's little secret: she is an alcoholic, a "functioning" one but an alcoholic nevertheless. The alcohol is her strategy to relieve her endurance, and her busyness is a cover-up for her real pain and fears. A few months ago, exhausted from her vicious cycle, Sharon had one of her periodic breakdowns and was hospitalized for a week. She told me that it was the best rest she had gotten all year: "No one bothered me. No one expected anything from me."

Sharon looks good to others and often earns rewards for her efforts, all the while suffering on the inside. But underneath it all, she is afraid she will be abandoned by her friends, her family, and even herself if she stops cultivating the image of the self-sacrificing woman whose integrity and standards no one would dare question. Sharon will remain trapped in her vicious cycle of do-gooding and exhaustion

1

so long as she focuses on her fears more than on her spirit's values and longings.

Sound at all familiar? Sharon is stuck in a perpetual cycle of endurance, feeling that she *must* continue with all of her good works—to the point of physical and emotional exhaustion—while never daring to question what is driving her behavior or how she might thrive in her life rather than just keep going "for the good of the team."

Symptoms of Endurance

Sharon's story certainly resonated for me. Even before my brain-tumor moment of truth, I identified a host of chronic habits—symptoms of endurance—that placed me squarely in Sharon's column:

- Always adding just one more thing to my to-do list
- Never feeling that I had time to stop
- Feeling panic at the thought that if I did stop, everything would fall apart
- Believing that it was hard enough to just survive, let alone thrive
- Feeling certain that others had more time than I would ever have
- Believing that I could never accomplish enough
- Distracting myself with eating, working, volunteering, cleaning
- Resenting that I never seemed to have enough time to do things that my spirit longed for
- Ignoring my feelings
- Taking responsibility for everything and everyone
- Hoping that someday this would all change and then I would pay attention to what I really wanted

What Keeps You Enduring

Endurance is what you experience when you think you don't have the right to whatever you feel or the right to choose an extraordinary life. Most of us succumb to a life of endurance with little resistance, if any. If we wake up most mornings feeling anxious, bored, or numb, looking toward some imagined future time when we will feel happier ("Once my children finally start school," "once I finally get my house organized," "once all my bills are paid off," "once I retire"), then we are enduring.

The Difference Between Surviving and Thriving

When we are enduring, we try to convince ourselves that surviving is the same as thriving. We tell ourselves that it should be *enough* that we made it through another day, earned our daily bread, performed our duties, and possibly helped others. But when we are merely surviving, we feel resigned, not inspired, exhausted but not accomplished. We know that *something* is missing, but we don't know exactly what or how to go about finding it.

Laura was a perfect example. When she first walked into my office, she had an air of resignation. She complained of feeling depressed. She told me flatly that she had two children and had been with the same man for fifteen years. "But my husband's my third child," she said, "I swear. He doesn't appreciate anything I do and he complains about everything. Why I picked him, I don't know."

It was time for the jackpot question: "How familiar does this relationship feel to you? Do you feel you've lived like this before?"

She thought for a moment and said, "Yeah, it's pretty familiar! When I was growing up, I learned that children are to be seen, not heard. In fact, if I gave my mother a hard time, she would grab my lips and twist them. Then she'd tell me she hadn't wanted me so I'd better make her want me now. She definitely let me know in a hundred ways that I wasn't appreciated."

"How do you feel about yourself now?" I asked Laura, curious.

"How do I feel about myself?" she laughed darkly. "What self? I think I decided a long time ago that I wasn't important." She sat for a minute and then shrugged. "If I think about it, I guess I'm scared most of the time."

I could see the fear in Laura's eyes. "What are you afraid of?"

"Everything, really. I'm afraid that my mother was right: that I'm not worth anything and I have to do everything for everybody so they'll want me. I figure that my only value is in being a better mother to my children than my mama was to me."

How Endurance Sneaks Up On You

Endurance, no matter how it manifests, is not living life but just marking time. Here's a scary thought: *endurance often looks and feels normal*, as it did to Laura.

Laura grew up feeling neglected and abused, and enduring such abuse was "natural" to her—she expected it. For Laura, the key to freeing herself was realizing that although her upbringing may have given her the blueprint for her endurance jail, she herself constructed the walls every day by fearing that she mattered only so long as she fulfilled other people's needs. I shared with her that for most of us, the two catch phrases while we are enduring are "Why me, Lord?" and "Is that all there is?" Laura laughed at these phrases, confessing that she said them out loud or thought them to herself every day.

Little by little, as we worked together, she began questioning her beliefs and fears. I explained that when we judge ourselves, we create endurance. If we continuously think *I'm fat* (*bad, stupid, ugly, unimportant*), how can we ever believe we are worthy of a good life, let alone an extraordinary one? Our unconscious limiting beliefs, such as "Others get to be happy, not me" or "The world is uncaring," interfere with our ability to thrive. Our fears and beliefs can keep us in confinement instead of allowing us to venture beyond our narrow borders. After considering this, she felt less inclined to want to continue believing her old thoughts anymore.

Laura worked conscientiously to be aware of these old thoughts and reject them when they came up. Soon, she began focusing instead on her spirit's desires, long buried under her old beliefs. Because she had always loved music, she decided to start taking piano lessons. She found it frightening at first to say no to the demands of her family and take an hour each day to practice playing piano, but she did it and loved it.

Her husband, who had learned to expect her to fulfill her role of endurance queen, was predictably angry about her new lack of attentiveness. "I tell you, Jane, he's throwing tantrums worse than my baby. But I'm the one who's let him get away with it, always taking care of him first. He'll either have to decide I'm important enough or I'm out of there." This was not the same Laura who had walked into my office ready to give in before she even spoke up for herself.

A few months later, they separated. Laura felt afraid that her old fears were true after all: maybe she was only worthwhile if she lived for others. Maybe she would be all alone if she focused on her own wants and needs. But after just three months of living apart, Laura's husband asked her if she would be willing to get back together again. She agreed—on condition that he go to counseling with her so that they could learn to create a healthier relationship.

For Laura (as for all of us), the end of her suffering began with noticing her chronic symptoms of endurance, and the fears and beliefs that kept her stuck with them.

🕐 Time In 🕐

Take another look at my list of symptoms of endurance,
and reflect on how your own endurance manifests itself.
How many of these habitual ways of behaving can you
identify in your own life? How do they affect
you and those who are important to you?

"Generosity" and Endurance

Laura was able to identify her symptoms of endurance as depression, resignation, and resentment. Sharon's—if only she could have identified them—were workaholism, overcommitment, and a feeling of martyrdom. Both women felt lethargic as they lived their lives, yet they believed that this was their lot. So they continued. And on it goes. In endurance, we resent time itself, feeling that there is never enough of it for us, that others somehow get more of it than we do, and that this imbalance will never cease.

Like Sharon, who was the epitome of a community volunteer, we are often exceptionally generous with our time, money, gifts, or listening skills. But in endurance, we have an unspoken contract with our recipients. Because we feel powerless, caught in a vicious cycle we do not understand, we secretly build up resentment. Eventually, we feel like martyrs ("After all I've done for you. . . ." "No one appreciates me around here."). Finally, something tips our scales and all the unconditional giving requires immediate payment. We suddenly view the recipients of our former generosity as accounts due. They usually don't know what hit them.

My client Nora told me that she thought of herself as trusting and generous. She and Gretchen had been friends for fifteen years, but Nora felt Gretchen took advantage of her.

"I lent her some money, and she never mentioned it again."

"What were the terms of your agreement?" I asked.

"We didn't really have any. I gave the money to her because I knew she was in a bind. I didn't want her to feel any pressure about it. But whenever I see her with a new dress on, I resent it. *I* could have bought a new dress with that money."

"Why haven't you brought this up with her?"

"Simple—I'm afraid that she'll think I'm stingy."

"Nora, because of this fear, you pretended there were no strings attached when you lent the money to Gretchen. But it seems you must have been judging yourself all along as not worthy of her friendship unless you give 'freely.'"

Deep down, Nora was afraid that Gretchen wouldn't want to be her friend if she didn't play the role of generous giver. Now Nora was a martyr from enduring so long. Ironically—as always happens when we make decisions on the basis of what we fear—Nora was getting precisely what she resisted. Her self-judgment was, "People don't really like me for who I am. I have to pay people to want to be friends with me." From her fear of being abandoned, she was creating the real possibility of losing a fifteen-year relationship.

When Nora spoke to Gretchen, she discovered that her friend had no idea that the money was a loan and not a gift. Gretchen felt embarrassed and asked Nora to be more truthful with her in the future about what she wanted. Nora promised she would.

Nora's generosity masked her fears of unworthiness and abandonment. She did not see that she was caught in a vicious cycle of fear turned into endurance, but at least she realized that her relationship with Gretchen was not healthy and that she was not thriving in it. This is a clue for all of us: whenever we are not thriving in some way, we must be enduring in some way. Once we recognize our symptoms and fears, we can begin to work with them.

Confusion and Endurance

People who live in endurance frequently feel confused about what they should be doing. This is because we are torn between listening to two inner voices: the voice of our spirit and the sometimes louder and more insistent one of our guardian self, which seeks to protect us from harm. Both have a role to play in our lives. Our spirit knows who we really are, what we really need, and how best to get it. Our guardian is in charge of making sure we survive in a world filled with danger and challenges. Ideally, the guardian keeps us from getting into the car to drive home after a night of drinking; or it may warn us, "There's something a little off about that person . . . let's avoid him."

The problem comes when, through some bad experience or trauma, this guardian voice gets stuck on a loud, attention-getting frequency (Watch out! Be careful!), seeing danger in every situation and around every corner.

Granted, there is a big job to do; ensuring our survival by protecting us from things that can hurt us keeps the guardian very busy. As we'll see, however, it can sometimes do its job too efficiently, seeing danger even where it doesn't exist while ignoring what would be in the best interests of our spirit. When our guardian's repeated dire warnings compete with our spirit's needs, which voice are we more likely to hear and heed?

Not surprisingly, then, many of us are not well acquainted with our spirit. We may even think of our spirit (our truer self) as somehow unreachable, the person we would be "if only I were braver." Our spirit may share its longings, but with our guardian self so loud we have to learn how to shift the attention to our spirit.

For example, I thought I was being a good person by taking care of my family and my clients. But by focusing almost exclusively on others instead of on my inner truth—my longing to write this book—I let my guardian self have total control and couldn't figure out why I wasn't feeling fully inspired. My spirit knew exactly what it wanted, but I was listening to the more insistent voice that was quite busy warning me about the possibility of failure. Our spirit whispers, "Aha! I know what I feel and want. And I am worthy of taking the risk to follow my dreams and aspirations." But our guardian self, fearing what might be out there, yells more loudly: "What you want is dangerous! Don't trust what you want. Don't trust your dreams or your intuition. Stick with me. I will keep you safe with these limiting beliefs and self-judgments."

How Endurance Disguises Itself

These conflicting voices create feelings and behaviors that are the hallmark of endurance: boredom, cynicism, hopelessness, depression, anxiety, confusion, annoyance, anger, frustration, resentment, busyness, addiction, melodrama. Because endurance often passes for what we think of as normal, we might misidentify and dismiss these symptoms, lumping them into the category of "stress."

We often treat these symptoms of endurance as separate problems; we take an antidepressant for the melancholy, or we practice yoga to decrease anxiety. We look for outside stimulation to counter our boredom or ignore nuances to avoid confusion. These strategies probably make us feel better, at least temporarily, but we may end up still feeling uninspired. If we avoid what our spirit longs for because we are listening to our guardian self's fears, we continue to endure in confusion. Endurance in all its disguises leads incrementally to spiritual death.

Keesha was confused about a lot of things in her life. When she first came to see me, she seemed even more nervous than a new client usually is, holding her hand over her mouth as she spoke. She said that she wanted to quit smoking cigarettes but was unable to stop. As she grew more comfortable with me, she told me her big secret: she had been bulimic since the age of twelve. She covered her mouth with her hand because her teeth were rotted from the acid left on them from frequent vomiting.

Keesha was genuinely confused about why she compulsively binged and purged and why she couldn't quit smoking. When I asked her to fill me in about her life, beginning at age twelve, Keesha told me that her father began molesting her just before she started her bulimic routine. She remembered feeling powerless because she didn't want to lose his love by saying no to him. Binging and purging, she would get a momentary feeling of control over her body that she didn't have when her father came into her room at night to fondle her. At age fourteen, in an attempt to stuff her shame and anger, she began smoking.

For the past thirty-five years, Keesha had told herself that she was confused about her behavior. In one hour, as she saw that her compulsive smoking and bulimia were symptoms of endurance, related to the fear of being abandoned by her father, she was able to find clarity. Eventually, Keesha gathered tremendous courage and confronted her father about molesting her. Steeling herself, she asked for an apology and for money to repair her teeth.

To her great surprise, Keesha's father not only apologized for molesting her and for making her life difficult in so many ways but also flew across the country to see me for a session. Such an event is rare, and noteworthy. Through the work we did, he realized that he too had been molested—by his grandmother. This discovery, this new truth, changed not only his life but Keesha's as well.

If we are confused, we do not know what our role is or should be. Keesha's underlying fear of abandonment by her father kept her confused and self-destructive. She felt loyal to her father and did not want to give up the role of devoted daughter. Her guardian self told her to play it safe and stay confused, even though the toll for staying in this role was quite high. Aware of this now, she lost the urge to continue the self-abusing pattern of bulimia. Her nicotine addiction was more difficult for her, but she stopped smoking completely a year later.

Clearly, Keesha's father was more helpful than many fathers are in such circumstances. Had he not opted to examine his own life of endurance and survival, Keesha might have had to face actual rejection and abandonment. But sometimes, as we gain clarity and muster the courage to face our fears, others take notice and become inspired, as Keesha's father was, to examine their fear and behavior and heal their emotional wounds.

Confusion wanes as we begin to see that our disguises of endurance have the same source. Keesha was a great example of the true source of endurance. Although she understood intellectually that she couldn't get out of her rut by focusing on her symptoms, like many people she thought that if her symptoms went away she would most certainly be happier. But until she valued herself and addressed her fear of abandonment, she could not free herself from the destructive habits she had practiced so long and so well.

How many times have you said, "If only this person loved me, I'd be happy" or "If only I had more money, I'd have no stress" or "If only I had more time, I'd exercise more, take a vacation, take that class . . ." and so on? In our confusion, we think "if only" and blame the world or ourselves for our unhappiness. This thinking keeps us stuck in a prison of endurance, feeling victimized and helpless. To get out of prison, we have to exchange our old, fear-based thoughts for new, more constructive ways of seeing the world and our place in it.

The Guardian Self's Motives

An alcoholic doesn't just quit drinking and start thriving, nor can a workaholic just stop working and be happy. If we don't deal with the sources of our endurance—our self-judgment and limiting beliefs that mask our true value as well as the fears that fuel these thoughts—it's Groundhog Day all over again. If we simply try to treat our symptoms, we exchange new symptoms for old ones.

All the fears that keep us in endurance can eventually cause us to live in resentment and regret for what might have been. Unless we live passionately, we come to resent life itself. Endurance continues only so long as we give our guardian self power over our spirit's deeper truth.

Regardless of the specifics, here's how a life of endurance gets its start:

1. In your childhood, an event or a series of events occurred that were painful or traumatic.

2. You feared that this pain would recur.

3. Your guardian was activated to help you avoid future pain and fear. It fed you self-judgments and limiting beliefs, which, although painful and stultifying, are the guardian's tools to keep you from risking further humiliation, hurt, rejection, and abandonment.

4. Over the years, your guardian continues to build evidence to reinforce your self-judgments and limiting beliefs. These thoughts gather strength and power until they develop into your self-image and your worldview.

5. Your life becomes a direct reflection—a mirror—of these thoughts. You behave according to your self-image and world-view, which you now believe to be the truth about yourself and the world. These behaviors are your survival strategies.

6. Your survival strategies—constantly reinforced by your guardian's fears, your evidence, and now your life experience—cause you to lose touch with your spirit's deeper truth.

7. You are enduring in ways you may not notice because endurance has come to seem both normal and inevitable.

🕐 Time In 🕐

Take some time to reflect on how your endurance came about. Can you identify a painful or traumatic childhood experience that led you to believe you are "damaged goods," or to believe that the world is frightening or cruel? How did you deal with your pain? How does this survival strategy still pop up in your life?

The Power of Your Spirit

Once we begin to understand that we are not just the sum total of our fears, self-judgment, limiting beliefs, and survival strategies, we find a way to live more richly and purposefully. If we pay attention to our spirit's messages, we begin to do things differently.

If your survival strategy has looked like doing too much for others, biting your tongue, avoiding confrontation, working too hard, or falling into an addictive pattern—all because you were afraid of being alone or abandoned—you can stop surviving and start thriving by changing your beliefs about yourself and what you deserve. As you listen to your spirit's truths and longings, you will realize that each day is a gift and a challenge to discover more of who you are becoming.

So who are you? You are a worthy human *being*, not merely an accumulation of fears, judgments, and limiting beliefs or all the things on your to-do list. You are unique and extraordinary. You will awaken to this truth by attending to your values, which stem from the dreams and aspirations of your spirit. This means putting the needs of your spirit first, and discovering what you value for yourself—beyond what you feel you need to do for others. For example, I discovered that I valued the challenge of writing. Laura discovered that she valued musical expression. Without the baggage of fear, Keesha made her truth and health a priority.

If we keep adding tasks to our to-do list without prioritizing them according to what really matters to our spirit, we will feel our symptoms of endurance. But by replacing our to-do list with a *to-be* list—one based on our truths rather than our "shoulds"—we thrive in the rhythm of our life and get to the really important stuff.

Tackling the important stuff tests our courage, yet our capacity to be inspired comes from knowing and living our values. We may even find that, by doing so, we discover we have more time for what matters most. If you have told yourself that you don't matter enough to make your life a priority, *take that back*. Try doing something you have held yourself back from doing. No one wants the epitaph on the grave to read, "She Completed Her To-Do List"!

 ### Process for Change
From To-Do List to To-Be List

First, take out your current to-do list:

1. What percentage of your list consists of chores, and what percentage consists of thriving activities?
2. How do you feel about this?

Now think about your to-be list:

1. Write down the activities (or note the absence thereof!) and goals that feed your spirit.

2. How many of them really come from deep inside you? How many instead reflect other people's expectations?

3. Cross off your list all the items that do not reflect your spirit's true longings and values.

4. Now prioritize your list according to your own passion and values.

5. How does your new list make you feel?

The Theory of Sunk Costs

Do you find this Process for Change exercise difficult? It can be hard to let go of endurance and make our own joy a priority. Sometimes it seems so much easier to keep throwing more resources into what we already know, *even if it isn't working.* In economics there is a theory known as sunk costs. These are the costs that have already been incurred and cannot be recovered no matter how much more is invested. Sunk cost theory states that one should not invest more just because a great deal has already been invested.

For example, if you buy a ticket to a play, the price of the ticket is a sunk cost. Now, let's say that between the time you purchase the ticket and curtain time you hear from a source you trust that the play is terrible. Do you go anyway, simply because you already paid for the ticket? If you are not aware of the theory of sunk costs, which says that costs that are not recoverable should not determine decision making, you might think you should endure the play anyway. But then you are throwing away both your money *and* your time. Your current decision should be based on whether you *want* to see the play, regardless of what you paid for the ticket, since the money is gone either way. Enduring by sitting through a terrible play on top of having paid the price of the ticket is irrational from the standpoint of both economics and psychology.

Have you ever stayed in a failing relationship because you already "invested" so much emotional energy? This emotional energy is a sunk cost. It is gone no matter what you do in the future. It is just as irrational to keep living in slavery to our fear-based limiting beliefs merely because we have done it for so long. If a thought has kept us in a rut, then sticking with it only wastes more of our time and our spirit's energy.

⏰   Time In   ⏰

Take a few minutes to think about a situation in which
you are continuing to invest more time, emotional energy,
or money simply because you have already invested a lot
previously. How does your fear-driven guardian voice argue
that you need to continue living with this decision?
What would your spirit prefer?

If you continue to invest in a relationship, a career, or even a lifestyle just because you have already spent so much on it, remember that whatever you spent is gone anyway. Don't waste one more minute or one more ounce of emotional energy on something that keeps you enduring. Become a volunteer, not a victim, by participating in your life consciously, sanely, and humanely.

❀ ❀

Here's the simple truth: if you are willing to question your old beliefs about yourself and the world, you can begin to experience a reality shift. As your mind changes, so does your world. Your spirit is still alive and knows exactly what you value, and what will inspire you to create your extraordinary life. The key to breaking free from your prison of endurance has been in your pocket all along. The key is your spirit's truth. You don't need to wait for someone else to open the door.

Chapter Two

Exit the Courtroom, Enter the Classroom

Let Go of Self-Judgments

Your worst enemy cannot harm you as much as your own thoughts.

—*The Dhammapada (ancient Buddhist text)*

On the eve of my wedding almost twenty years ago, I felt a surprising panic wash over me. Until that night, I felt very excited and joyous. But our buttons—the triggers of our unconscious self-judgments—are often pushed at the strangest moments, regardless of outward circumstances. I took my sudden panic as a sign that I should not go through with the ceremony. I sat my fiancé down and told him that I couldn't marry him. In his shock and confusion, of course he asked me why. I couldn't answer; I only knew that I wanted to run for the hills. After hours of putting myself and my soon-to-be-but-almost-wasn't husband through the wringer, I came to my bottom line: I believed I didn't deserve him because of my "sordid" past. I thought of myself as damaged goods—a broken egg, like Humpty Dumpty, who could never be put back together again.

Luckily, he was buying none of this. As I sobbed and confessed every sin and shortcoming, offering him evidence of my unworthiness, certain that he would agree that I was not marriage material, he just stroked my hair and reminded me that he knew most of this stuff already.

After so many years of contentment in a loving marriage, I can look back at this melodrama of mine and feel compassion for myself. How powerful my self-judgment was! I sometimes find it hard to believe that I made such a serious attempt at rejecting my husband so that I could avoid his rejecting me in the future.

How to End Up On Trial

Here's what happened: I assumed that my panic was a message of truth from my spirit to cancel the wedding, when it was actually a self-judgment conceived by my overprotective guardian to save me from some anticipated future hurt. I have since learned the key to distinguishing between the messages of my spirit and those of my guardian: *any message that is not filled with self-worth and compassion is a self-judgment, not a truth from my spirit.* With this awareness, I am much better equipped to identify my self-judgments, question their validity, and let them go.

Since it is impossible to expel our guardian self on command (or even sometimes at will), we are obligated to get to know it better and make it our ally. Had I recognized my panic as a message from my guardian, I'm sure I would have been much less harsh with myself and easier to console. Had I remembered that self-accusation must always come from my guardian, I would have said, "Guardian, thank you for sharing. Now, spirit, where do you stand on this one?" I might have then been able to hear the truth more quickly: without question, I wanted to marry this wonderful man who comforted me so lovingly.

The Truth About Self-Judgment

Your self-judgment is real—you certainly experience its power in your life. But your numerous judgments are not *true* because they do not reflect your intrinsic value as a human being.

Your self-judgment involves not just honest appraisal but condemnation and reproach for who you *believe* you are. "I'm too stupid (or ugly, or pathetic, or fat, or skinny)" are typical self-judgments. They are usually followed by admonitions such as "I should lose weight (or work harder or learn more quickly)" Whether or not you formulate your self-judgments using this exact wording, they probably all contain the word *too* or *should*. Anytime we think we are *too* anything, or we *should* do something we are not doing or being, we can be absolutely certain we are judging.

The original voice of our self-judgment almost always belongs to someone from our childhood: a parent, caretaker, relative or friend, teacher, even a casual acquaintance. As children, we naturally trust others to know more about us than we do, and to know what's true. So if, for example, your father called you stupid as a child, you may have adopted this judgment and then acted on what you perceived as fact. If your mother said you were a bother, you may have taken what could have been a random comment, spoken in a moment of impatience, as a truth that you are a burden to everyone in your life. If some classmates shunned you in the fifth grade, you may still feel insecure about your popularity.

Not surprisingly, the survival strategies we develop as children to handle fear, hurt, pain, and trauma tend to be childlike and naïve. Generally, we are apt to think that if things go wrong, it's somehow "our fault" (a self-judgment) or that "this is just the way the world is" (a limiting belief). If we are fortunate enough to have adults around us to disabuse us of these mistaken ideas, we can move on to a more sophisticated understanding of the world and our place in it. But if our self-blaming thoughts are reinforced by those who have authority over us as children, we can end up carrying these thoughts with us and feel "like a trunk going through an airport, covered in stickers," as the actress Kim Basinger noted.

These stickers—our self-judgments—are lies that ferment into quasi-truths as we live them out. For example, if you were treated in a way that made you think you were of little value and have thus come to judge yourself as unworthy of respect, you may settle for less than total respect in relationships, work, or friendship. Does this mean that you do not deserve respect? Of course not. But if you have based your life on such a painful judgment, you may readily accept others treating you with incivility and disregard.

We see a skewed, catawampus reality through the lens of our self-judgment—just as, for example, an anorexic does. Even though she steps on the scale and sees it register eighty-five pounds, as she looks in the mirror she sees a "fat" girl—not the frighteningly skeletal figure her friends and family see. Why? Because she is filtering out all information that is inconsistent with her distorted self-judgment.

Laila had this distorted view of herself. Rejected ten years ago by a high school boyfriend who thoughtlessly called her "pudge," she had come to believe she was too fat to be loved. Every time Laila felt rejected by a man, she found evidence that it was her body that made her unlovable. To make matters worse, whenever a man did show her attention, she distrusted him immediately. Unconsciously, she was colluding with Groucho Marx's humorous but self-deprecating remark: "I don't care to belong to a club that accepts people like me as members."

By the time Laila came for coaching, she was desperately lonely. Her outfit—an oversized man's shirt and sweatpants—hid her body and effectively sent the message, "I am not interested in attention." To top it off, she kept her thick auburn hair pulled back in a ponytail. All of this was conscious. She told me bluntly, "I dress like this so I won't be noticed."

"But if you don't get noticed," I pointed out gently, "you will keep believing that you are too fat to be loved."

"But if I *do* get noticed and then rejected, I will *really* believe it."

"You seem to already believe it," I replied. "So aren't you stopping yourself from ever finding out that you might be wrong?"

I suggested to Laila that maybe the real problem wasn't her weight, which looked to be close to the range of normal anyway, but the message she was sending to men by how she dressed.

"Yeah," she agreed after a while, "you're probably right. I do want them to stay away from me because I'm pretty sure they'll hurt me." She was silent for a long time, thinking. "But really, I'm hurting myself with my own thoughts *all the time*." With this realization, she broke down in sobs.

At our next session, Laila seemed to have reached new clarity of purpose. She was still wearing the big clothes, but her beautiful hair was swinging free and she told me that she had come to a decision: "I've decided to get a makeover from head to toe—hair, facial, massage, personal shopper—just like on TV."

Once she started paying some attention to herself, Laila began to feel less negative; maybe there was hope after all. She certainly felt better about the way she looked, and she observed that once she felt better about herself, men seemed to take more notice of her. She recognized, though, that she still had to fight hard against her instinct to distrust their intentions.

"Maybe you need to get to know some men as friends before you feel comfortable becoming more intimate," I suggested. As Laila began to feel comfortable in her own skin, she reached out to more men and began seeing them as individuals, not as a stereotype. Slowly, her suspiciousness ebbed as her interest in particular men grew.

Laila had spent years putting her energy into hiding herself from pain, and she paid a price for this protection: she sacrificed deeper connection by stereotyping and she lost touch with who she really was or wanted to be. The more resources we invest in self-judgment and limiting beliefs, the fewer resources we have left in service of our spirit.

Fortunately, Laila was able to learn the difference between honest self-appraisal and hurtful self-judgment. But in our culture of self-improvement, this is not always the normal course of events. Many (if not most) of us try to "improve" ourselves using the same weapon that is destroying us: we try to fix what we perceive as wrong with ourselves by judging ourselves more harshly. We drive ourselves harder, and we end up feeling more frustrated or hopeless. This vicious cycle leads to endurance that goes on and on and on.

If we attempt to cure whatever we judge in ourselves through harsh remedies, we continue finding new faults "requiring" even more severe treatment. If we fail to live up to our ever-more-stringent standards, we admonish ourselves so fiercely for failing that we could just as well place a sign on our chest reading, "Enemies need not apply. Vacancy filled."

Stop the Torture

So, what can we do instead? We can learn to question the validity of our exhaustive list of negative thoughts and beliefs, assess their damaging effect, and discover what is truer. Even though we have spent a lifetime stockpiling evidence that validates our worst thoughts, like Laila we can stop.

Martin, a forty-one-year-old retail manager, stockpiled evidence of his inadequacy for years. Intelligent and capable, he had risen up the corporate ladder four times, only to lose each job after he reached upper management. He told me that he felt ashamed of being unemployed and was embarrassed to send his resume to prospective employers: "I know these companies can smell my failure. I should be at the top by now, not applying for these intermediate positions."

"How have you managed to lose all these jobs?" I wondered. Martin struck me as a great guy—funny, smart, and ready to work.

"Well, eventually, I clashed with every one of my bosses. Then I'd leave before they could fire me. Maybe I just have authority issues," he said halfheartedly.

But I wanted to know why Martin felt ashamed and embarrassed about his employment. He sat with the feelings for a while and then blurted out suddenly, "I think it's because of my cat."

I've learned that the thread connecting early life experience and current difficulty is not always obvious, so I waited for him to continue.

Filled with shame, Martin whispered that at nineteen he had abandoned his cat after it scratched and bit him. Rather than bring it to the pound or try to find a home for it, he drove the cat to the other side of town and abandoned it in a field. An animal lover at heart, he never told anyone and never forgave himself for it.

I believed that this decision, seemingly so unlike the Martin I had come to know, could only be explained by some deeper, earlier pain.

When I gently asked if he could connect this act of abandonment to anything in his childhood, he replied in a small voice, "My mother left me when I was six." As a young boy, he had come to believe that he must have done something horrible and that he did not deserve his mother's love—or anyone else's either. Although he earned good grades in school and had his share of friends, at nineteen he unconsciously replayed his own childhood pain by abandoning his cat. "But that's no excuse for leaving my cat like that," he protested.

"It happened," I replied. "At least let that recognition be a starting place for some clarity and self-forgiveness. Have you ever abandoned another animal since then?"

"Never! I could never forgive myself."

"But Martin, if you continue to judge yourself so harshly, you're just going to keep sabotaging your career."

With his cat story out in the open, Martin finally came to see that his shame and belief in his unworthiness originated with his mother's abandonment and that keeping himself in a prison of shame was only going to lead to more misery. His life didn't change miraculously overnight, but his pattern of leaving a job just when he would snag an upper management position *did* change. He stopped blaming his bosses or issues about authority and stopped undermining his success.

⏰ Time In ⏰

Take a moment to reflect on the real impact of
self-judgment on yourself and others. Recall a time
when you looked in your mirror in the morning in self-
judgment, telling yourself that you were fat, ugly, old,
stupid, worthless, unlovable, whatever. How did this
thought affect your day? How did you behave toward
others on the basis of these thoughts? How did the
world mirror back to you your beliefs about yourself?
In other words, how did others treat you in return?

Exposing the Big Lie

The core thought underlying Martin's and Laila's self-judgments is common to most of us: I am unworthy. We say to ourselves, "I'm unworthy because . . ." and give some reason or set of reasons for how we fall short. I'm unworthy because I had an abortion. I'm unworthy because I didn't go to graduate school. I'm unworthy because I let myself be abused. I'm unworthy because I can't keep the house clean. I'm unworthy because I lied in a past relationship. I'm unworthy because I abandoned someone or something. I'm unworthy because I was abandoned by my mother or father. I'm unworthy because I don't exercise enough. But the specific way we complete this sentence is immaterial. It is the *I am unworthy* part of the sentence that is the lie. Like Martin, we then reinforce the lie that we are unworthy by behaving in ways that mirror this belief.

What we think, we come to believe. What we believe, we manifest through our behavior, and our world reflects our beliefs back to us. So just by pulling off our "stickers"—banishing our self-judgment— we can readjust the distorted lens through which we view the world and begin to break free of endurance.

The foundation of all my work with clients is this core premise: *we are worthy, extraordinary beings deserving of love, forgiveness, and compassion, particularly from ourselves.* I believe that no therapy, spiritual counseling, or healing can be effective without embracing this belief.

If we are willing to believe in our worthiness, we can heal our addiction, our sabotaging behavior, and our covert and overt abuse of others and ourselves. If we pull off our stickers—our self-judgments— we can break the vicious cycle that keeps us enduring.

To the degree we cling to our self-judgment, we cannot take in love. How can we receive love that we do not believe we deserve? How can we allow love in when we look in the mirror and see damaged goods? In self-judgment, love becomes tenuous. We are afraid there is not enough of it out there, but in fact, it is the love inside that is missing. I had to learn this the hard way: I pushed love away on the eve of my marriage because I judged myself as unworthy. Remember, every self-judgment is based on a lie—the lie that we are unworthy.

🕐 Time In 🕐

Just for a moment, believe that it is true
that you are worthy. How do you feel?

The fear underlying our self-judgment is that we will be abandoned by others because we are unworthy. All our fears come down to this one fear that keeps us in prison. It keeps us from risking, from opening our hearts more, from recognizing our own loving nature, and from letting others love us.

Find a New Identity

If self-judgments weigh us down so heavily, why isn't it easier to just drop them and move on? One reason is that criticizing ourselves is habit-forming. Like any habit, we have to decide that we are worthy of the effort to break an old habit and practice new behavior. Although we might think we would be instantly relieved to know that we were wrong about our judgments and limiting beliefs, it can be frightening to let go of them. After all, they have given us a set of decisions and an identity (false as it may be) that offer some degree of comfort.

For example, if you have come to believe that you are not smart enough, then you may decide not to pursue more education. Holding onto this belief keeps you from risking failure. So your decision brings you a kind of comfort, even though you may be bored and miserable in your job.

But the urge for safety comes with a price. Every time we protect ourselves from the possibility of pain, we also protect ourselves from the possibility of intimacy, healing, and inspiration. By holding the "safe" belief that we are undeserving or not good enough in any way, we create financial, emotional, or spiritual poverty. So the decision to stop one's education might result in enduring a boring, dead-end job.

We carry our judgments around with us to protect our vulnerability, like a turtle carries its shell. This shell of self-judgment shields us from potential harm, but it is also confining. We point to our judgments and say, "Can't you see? I've got this and that wrong with me. These things stop me from achieving and from being happy." Hiding underneath our self-judgment may offer justification for our fears and limitations, but it effectively precludes us from leading an extraordinary life. This was a lesson that Mariko learned at the age of thirty.

Mariko was the middle child of three daughters. She was expected to do well in school, but her parents never put pressure on her to do her best. Mariko believed this was because her older sister (now a doctor and always a high achiever in school) had already filled the role of "the star" in the family. Mariko learned not to make waves and put herself through school to become a dental hygienist.

But this "invisible" girl wasn't the real Mariko. "I feel restless, Jane. I'm bored to death cleaning people's teeth. I want more out of life." She looked miserable. "I guess I just don't know how to get more, though. I get really excited about trying new things—dance classes, art classes—but everyone else in the class is just so much better and younger than I am. Maybe I should have started earlier. I don't know. Anyway, if I can't do it really well, whatever it is, why bother?"

"Oh Mariko, that's so sad! Do you have any longings right now?"

Mariko responded in a tiny voice. "I want to be an artist—and not just a starving one. I want to design book jackets." I was startled that Mariko had such a specific goal in mind.

"But I would have to be accepted by the art institute and take courses, and then I would have to work as an apprentice for little or no pay." She raised her eyes and looked at me intensely. This was a moment of choice for Mariko, and she knew it.

Mariko knew that reaching her goal—leaving endurance behind and thriving as the *real*, extraordinary Mariko—would mean leaving behind her protective shell of self-judgment. Like Mariko, most of us have carried around our self-judgments since childhood, yet we still listen to them as though this is the first time we were hearing them. More disturbingly, we tend to trust them more than we trust compliments or self-acknowledgment.

⏰ Time In ⏰

What risk have you avoided taking because it might lead to potential failure or rejection? What reasons have you used to stop yourself from taking this risk? What would you be doing *right now* if you were not letting your self-judgment keep you from taking this risk?

After six more months of restlessness and frustration, Mariko took a risk and applied to the art institute. As seems always to be the case when someone takes the risk to listen to the spirit's yearnings, a world of possibilities quickly opened up. One of her professors recognized her talent, enthusiasm, and maturity and asked her if she would like to join the faculty after completing his class. Mariko, so unaccustomed to being the star, could hardly believe that she stood out in a crowd of very talented students. Nevertheless, in her second year at the art institute, Mariko was both a part-time design instructor and a full-time student.

From Courtroom Earth to Classroom Earth

By now, you may have realized that all of your self-judgments contribute to your stay in endurance jail. Putting ourselves on trial, prosecuting ourselves, and meting out a harsh sentence for our "offense," we don't need others' judgment—we are our own judge, jury, and executioner. This is what it is like to live in Courtroom Earth (an expression I heard and embraced years ago).

Fortunately, we are entitled to live in an alternative and much more humane universe: Classroom Earth, where we are allowed to question the authority of our judgments, make mistakes, and give ourselves compassion. It's plausible to think that getting from Court-room Earth to Classroom Earth is a long journey, but in fact, we can walk out of one room and into the other instantly, with just a little preparation and practice. Here's how Amanda found her way from the courtroom to the classroom.

Amanda visited with family—her parents, two brothers, their wives and children—on special occasions, which included relatives' birthdays and holidays. It was very difficult for her to be around one sister-in-law, Josie. "I swear, that woman looks forward to ruining Thanksgiving every year," she told me, tapping her toe impatiently. "She causes a fight and looks for trouble. I can't stand her! She flies into rages, she demands special attention—and to top it off, she never helps with cooking or dishes. She acts like a princess expecting to be served." Amanda was livid with her sister-in-law. Who wouldn't be? But she was also frustrated with herself for never confronting Josie.

Amanda's feeling of helplessness in the situation puzzled her. She couldn't understand why she had tolerated this behavior for so many years without ever speaking up. She had to look into her childhood to figure this one out. I wondered if anything about this felt familiar.

"I guess so," she reluctantly admitted. "My parents fought a lot. I hated to hear them and was afraid they would eventually divorce. My role in the family was to calm my parents down. I would beg them to stop fighting, and I would promise them anything—that I'd be a better daughter, that I'd do dishes, take the dog for a walk, any-thing to get them to stop. Sometimes it worked. They actually did stop fighting."

So Amanda grew up believing she had the power to stop dissent in the family. On the face of it, this sounds empowering. How did it turn out to be limiting? Paradoxically, she came to see easing tension as her burden, and if it didn't happen it was her fault. So Josie's tirades were a trigger for Amanda's helplessness and self-judgment that she wasn't doing enough to keep the peace. No wonder she was so frustrated.

As Amanda and I talked about Courtroom Earth and Classroom Earth, she saw that whenever Josie disrupted an event with an outburst, Amanda immediately put *herself* on trial. She was motivated to find the way out of the courtroom and into the classroom.

First, she consciously decided to stop taking responsibility for keeping the peace. Then she decided she might be able to overcome her helpless feelings by confronting Josie about her behavior. Without waiting for the next family gathering, Amanda got up all of her nerve and asked Josie to meet her for coffee and talk about their relationship. To her surprise, Josie agreed. "Josie," she began in a nervous rush, "I'm so uncomfortable with your temper. It reminds me of my parents fighting when I was growing up, and I don't want to be around that anymore. I know I can't change your moods, but I can choose to leave when you have a tantrum—*and I will*." She stopped to catch her breath. "Also, I should have told you before, but I have been resentful of you for not helping out at our family dinners. I feel like your slave, not your sister-in-law."

Amanda waited for Josie to start screaming at her, but instead, she burst into tears. She told Amanda that she had never felt embraced as part of Amanda's family. Amanda was taken aback and encouraged Josie to talk about it with other family members instead of continuing to act on this premise. As tactfully as possible, she pointed out that Josie had created a self-fulfilling prophecy of not being welcomed by behaving so outrageously. Josie apologized to Amanda, who went home relieved and absolutely stunned at this turn of events. Things really did work differently in Classroom Earth. At the next family dinner, Josie helped without asking, reaching out to the family she had so feared would reject her.

The best chance of getting someone else to change his or her behavior toward us is to change our own behavior. If we simply stop trying the case against ourselves in the courtroom and are therefore more introspective and vulnerable, those who might usually react defensively often respond to us less guardedly. By being truthful with Josie about her feelings, Amanda created an environment where Josie could feel safer. In Classroom Earth, both women had the experience that they could be truthful and calm their inner guardians' urges to attack and defend, in a way they could never have done in Courtroom Earth.

Question Authority

Beverly, a talented writer, discovered that what is revealed can be healed. As soon as she questioned her mother's authority and the validity of her own beliefs, she began to feel empowered.

When Beverly first came to coaching, she was struggling with money issues. She was vivacious and the winner of many writing awards, but she still lived the life of a starving artist who doubted her own talent. When we talked about her childhood, I learned that her parents had never married, and her father left before she was in kindergarten, offering no financial support to Beverly's mother and their four children. The budget in Beverly's family was beyond tight. Her writing talent showed itself early on, but her pragmatic mother wasn't impressed. "Anybody can scribble something on paper," she often told her daughter. "It takes a lot of talent to turn those words into food on the table."

"I believed my mom, of course," Beverly told me. "She was the only adult I could count on. She was wise, in my eyes. But I definitely got the message that if I don't have financial comfort at any given time, this must be a reflection of my talent . . . or lack of it. When I don't know where my next paycheck is coming from, I can't help but think my mom was right."

"So even though you've had the courage to follow your dreams of becoming a writer, you still don't believe you have enough talent to be financially comfortable?"

"Not really. Not when there's no money in the bank and the credit card bill is due."

"Tell me about your mom's childhood. What did she grow up believing?"

"She grew up during the Depression, when jobs were scarce. She was artistic too but had to help support her family by being a seamstress. I guess she gave up on being an artist."

"It sounds as though her decision might have been based on a number of factors: her evaluation of her own talent, the messages she got from her family, as well as the economy and culture of the time. It seems to me that you have taken her self-judgment and limiting beliefs as gospel instead of recognizing that they could be based on her personal story and experiences."

Beverly had never thought of it this way. As she began to understand that the rules her mother grew up with might not be valid for her own life, and that she was using finances as a way to reinforce her self-judgment and limiting beliefs, she began to break free of her vicious cycle. The first step was to quit assessing her writing ability according to her earnings.

Self-judgments play such a large role in our lives because we are continuously reinforcing them with our behavior. But what if we simply pull the plug?

Beverly needed to stop giving so much credence to her self-judgment and limiting beliefs. If she had insufficient funds to cover the credit card bill when it came due, she could acknowledge her negative thoughts, give them a few minutes of her time, and then shoo them away.

Interestingly, Beverly became more financially successful as a writer as she believed more in her talent and less in her limiting beliefs. Questioning authority freed her muse.

By giving less power to our negative thoughts, we step out of Courtroom Earth and into Classroom Earth. Once we say yes to learning instead of to prosecution and punishment, we no longer need to defend against or hide from our self-judgment. The irony is that, through acceptance, we become the better people we tried to become while berating ourselves with our self-judgment!

Time Off for Good Behavior

Many of us have learned that we must first change our thoughts in order to change our behavior. However, the opposite strategy can be just as powerful—and quite a bit easier. Change your behavior and your thoughts just might follow. By practicing new ways of behaving, you can calm your guardian and downsize your self-judgment. By behaving in accordance with your values, you will come to believe the truth that you are a worthy being.

 ### Process for Change
Behaving As If

1. Think about a self-judgment you have. It could be about your intellect, your looks, your maturity, the amount of money you make or spend, your level of honesty, how you treat your children—anything that bothers you about yourself. How do you act from your self-judgment? (For example, if your self-judgment is that you're not frugal enough, you may alternate between scrimping and binge spending.)

2. Now think: How would you behave if you were no longer judging yourself in this way? (You might create a budget that allows some "play money.") Write down all the ways in which you would act differently.

3. For today, practice these behaviors and see how your self-judgment diminishes.

Although we have every right to remedy something we do not like in ourselves, such as our weight, our temperament, or even our ignorance, we can focus on practicing new behavior to change not only how we treat others but how we treat ourselves.

Revise Your Story

As the stories in this book make abundantly clear, we learn who we supposedly are (and are not) from a very early age—which means that if we never examine our childhood decisions, then we are giving our seven-year-old complete control over our lives!

Over time, our self-judgments become so ingrained that we often don't realize that they even exist, or that they deserve to be questioned. On the basis of messages from our childhood, we also learn what we are supposedly capable of and what should be considered out of the question for us. For example, if your mother thought she was poor at art and looked at your painting and said "You're just like me," that was a judgment you may not question to this day. If you came home with a C on a spelling test and your father said jokingly, "Another creative speller in the family," that could have been enough to convince you that you would always have a problem with spelling.

Your story contains clues about your self-judgments and limiting beliefs and is of utmost importance because you have interpreted the world through it. Your beliefs, the messages you learned about yourself, your ideas about relationships—everything is right there in your story.

It is time to rethink your story. As an adult, you have perspective that you could not possess as a child living out your story. And every story has alternative viewpoints.

Like Phil in *Groundhog* Day, if we continue to tell ourselves the same tired story—the one with all our self-judgment and limiting beliefs in it—we get stuck re-creating the same monotonous day. We will feel that poet Edna St. Vincent Millay's statement is right: "It's a mistake to think of life as one damned thing after another. It's the same damned thing over and over." But this statement reflects resignation that stems from regurgitating our self-judgment and limiting beliefs. Reviewing our story from a fresh angle frees us to allow today and tomorrow to be different from yesterday.

🕐 Time In 🕐

Think about a time in your childhood that still feels
painful in some way. Is there a self-judgment or limiting
belief you hold from that time? Examine your story
again from an adult perspective. What is the essential
quality that got you through this: courage?
forgiveness? intuition? cleverness?

In addition to finding the self-judgment and limiting beliefs in our stories, we can also learn to see others from our past differently. Our empathy for others may grow, or we may become angry with someone for the first time. Thoughts and beliefs we accepted unconditionally may become a little more suspect.

Perhaps the greatest value in revisiting our story is to stop living a life that is defined by others' beliefs about us. Until we review our own story, we may still be acting out others' expectations of us. These expectations may be grand, or they may be minimal. But if they are not aligned with our own spirit's values and longings, we are not living an authentic, extraordinary life. How can we know who we really are if we still define ourselves by opinions and judgment imposed on us as small children? Whatever new perspectives we gain, our story has the power to reveal to us insights that, as children, we could not fathom.

The One Rule That Will Set You Free

We have suffered enough for our self-judgment! As the Jewish sage Hillel said, "What is hateful to you, do not do to your neighbor. That is the whole Torah." Let's add a corollary: "What is hateful to you, do not do to yourself." *Judgment is hateful to you.* Begin to heal self-judgment and limiting beliefs by offering yourself compassion.

For much of my life, I believed I should not become a mother. I was afraid for many reasons. I feared that I could not love a child as much as I loved my pets. I feared that I would hurt a child emotionally by getting too angry. Most of all, I judged myself as not having the skills needed to do the job well. However, with plenty of reassurance from my husband and close friends, I eventually took the plunge, and although I adore my daughter I am not always the perfect mother. But when she points out my errors (as children do), I have two choices: locked in my self-judgment and fear I can defend myself and then attack her, hoping to confuse her and deflect any responsibility from myself. Or I can acknowledge my behavior and apologize as quickly as possible.

Without compassion for myself, I have the tendency to cling to my fear that I must appear to be right or she will not love me. When I offer myself compassion for my mistakes, I feel remorse for my behavior and let my spirit guide me back to the closeness I share with my daughter.

If we offer ourselves compassion, our judgment eases its grip on us, creating room for something new to take its place. We can choose to fill this space with affirming thoughts that we are willing to practice believing. An affirmation is a statement of intention. We phrase an affirmation not as a wish or dream, but as if it is already true. We may not yet believe it, but we are *willing* to believe it.

For example, you can create an affirmation that says, "I, [use your name], now believe I am worthy and behave accordingly." Or you can have an affirmation that says, "I, _____ , now give myself the respect and care that I want others to give to me." Another great affirmation is, "I, _____ , am enough and have always been enough. All thoughts to the contrary have been an illusion."

If you have ever had the good fortune of someone believing in you more than you believed in yourself, then you understand just how powerful positive thoughts are. If someone else sees something in us that we have not yet seen in ourselves, we may achieve beyond our imagination. Affirmations work the same way. Using the power of our thoughts to demonstrate belief in our potential, we can also heal and achieve beyond our imagination.

Pickle and Jelly Sandwiches

Some people complain that affirmations and the power of positive thinking don't work or are spiritual mumbo-jumbo. But this skepticism is like complaining about still tasting pickles in a sandwich if all we have done is cover them with jelly. Unless we are committed to *removing* the pickles before putting on the jelly, we will keep tasting pickles. We must remove our self-judgment and limiting beliefs in order to taste the sweet results of our affirmations.

Have you ever heard the twelve-step program phrase, "Fake it till you make it"? This is not encouragement to act inauthentically; it is encouragement to expand our imagination about who we are. If you want to become more inspired, then "talk the talk" and "walk the walk" of an inspired person. Most inspired people aren't born that way; they recognize their fear and self-judgment but choose to listen to their spirit, thereby practicing becoming who they wish to be. If we are willing to hold a new thought about ourselves, even for a day, we will surely find evidence for this new thought. If we can be open to the evidence and not consider it an exception to the rule, we will start to question the old authority of our self-judgment and limiting beliefs and, most important, change our own mind.

 ### Process for Change
Releasing Self-Judgment

1. Sit down with a piece of paper and a pencil. Write every self-judgment you have, including the harshest and most embarrassing ones. Take at least fifteen minutes to write down all your self-judgments.

2. Check in with how you feel right now: ashamed? burdened? sad? Are you bored with any of the judgments?

3. Rip up your self-judgments and burn them as a symbol of your willingness to let go of these illusions and to stop creating evidence for them.

4. Offer yourself compassion for having carried the burden of your self-judgments.

5. Replace your judgments with affirmations. Put your name in them, and set them in present time.

   Examples:

   "I, _____ , now recognize my worth."

   "I, _____ , now create loving relationships."

   "I, _____ , am worthy of getting my degree."

Be willing to believe them. Find new evidence to support them. They are as true as you allow them to be.

❀ ❀

Each day we live, we have a choice. The choice to continue torturing ourselves with self-judgment creates war within us and between us. The choice to release ourselves from the tyranny of these thoughts creates peace. Every day, we create either war or peace. We endure or we thrive. We live an ordinary life or an extraordinary one. Which do you choose today?

Chapter Three

Remove Your Blinders

See Without Limiting Beliefs

> The first thing you have to realize is that you are in
> prison. If you think you are free, you can't get out.
> —G. I. *Gurdjieff*

"I'm so frustrated with my life!" Betsy told me. When I asked her why, she reeled off a list of reasons.

At thirty-five, she had already risen high up the corporate ladder. Now she wanted to get married and have a family. So she went out once a week with her girlfriends to have fun and meet men— even though she didn't like bars, was uncomfortable with flirting and making small talk, and felt rejected when she tested the waters with men and received no response.

"It's impossible," she wailed, bemoaning her fate. "There aren't any good, single men out there. I should just face up to the fact that I'll never find a relationship. I know there are more single women out there than men. Maybe I'm fooling myself thinking that I need a partner and a family to complete my life."

When I asked Betsy if she recognized how many limiting beliefs she had just rattled off, she bristled, clinging valiantly to them while denying they were beliefs. She shot back, "What I have are facts. Fact one: it is almost impossible to find a decent, single man after a woman reaches thirty-five. Fact two: this town has a poor ratio of single men to single women. Fact three: all the good men are taken. Fact four: the pickup scene in bars is disgusting. I would never date a man I met at a bar." Betsy had even gathered statistics from a magazine supporting some of her claims and insisted that I look at the data.

"OK, OK!" I cried. "You have all your evidence that you will never get what you want. But since that doesn't make you want it any less, I suggest you shift your attention. Instead of building more evidence, how about finding articles about women who were thirty-five and over who did find loving relationships? How about seeking out couples who met each other at your age?"

"Oh, come on," she said. "I really doubt I'm going to find a lot of real-life stories like that."

"Simply be willing, Betsy. You may discover things happening just outside your peripheral vision, if you're open to seeing them."

"Alright," she said, "but I'll bet I don't find anything."

Betsy was sure that she would have little to report, but two weeks later—much to her surprise—she had three stories of thirty-something women who had found partners. She felt inspired enough to try a tactic that worked for two of the women: they met their part-ners in dance classes. Since Betsy loved to dance, she decided she would take salsa lessons. Before she left my office, I asked her to cre-ate an affirmation that would remind her of her willingness to have what she wanted.

"OK. 'I, Betsy, am willing to meet my future husband now.' How's that, Jane? I think this is hokey, but I am desperate," she laughed.

As they say, desperation is the mother of invention. With that in mind, Betsy began her dance classes.

She did not meet the man of her dreams in her salsa class. But the fun and joy of dancing revived her spirit, and she found herself opening up more. Ironically, she ended up meeting her boyfriend in a bar—the very place she had rejected as a possible environment for finding love.

Think Outside the Box

Betsy had hung onto her limiting beliefs for dear life when what she needed was to let go of them to have that dear life. Once she was able to see that her limiting beliefs might not be true, her world opened up. Her experience was not an aberration. As the philosopher Arthur Schopenhauer wisely observed, "All truth passes through three stages. First, it is ridiculed. Second, it is violently opposed. Third, it is accepted as being self-evident."

By tenaciously holding to the belief that the world works in one particular way, or that there is only one right way to do something, or that our actions will inevitably result in a specific and predictable outcome, we strap on blinders that don't allow us to see anything except what we have always seen.

As our willingness to think outside the box (our own box) expands, we often see the world change before our eyes. Until May 6, 1954, for example, no one had ever been recorded running a mile in under four minutes. Most experts, runners, and fans believed it was impossible for a human being to run that fast. But Roger Bannister, trained as an athlete and as a physician, wanted to prove that the impossible was possible. That day, on a track in England, the twenty-five-year-old Bannister ran the mile in 3:59.4, simultaneously shattering not just an old speed record but an old limiting belief. Less than two months later, another athlete broke the barrier. Soon after, a *third* performed this feat. Bannister himself bettered his own achievement that same year. In 1994, Eamonn Coghlan ran the mile in 3:58.15, beating Bannister's initial record. Coghlan was forty-one years old.

Old rules crumble as we open to possibilities. But this can trigger our guardian self once more, putting us right back into our prison of familiar discomfort.

The Trap of Familiarity

Our self-judgment sends us into endurance, and our limiting beliefs make sure we stay there. We believe that we *must* keep doing what we have been doing because *that's just the way life is*. Sounds bleak, doesn't it? But if we didn't get something out of it, we wouldn't keep doing it. Paradoxically, what we often get—no matter how miserable we are—is a feeling of familiarity and safety. We tell ourselves that the devil we know is better than the one we don't.

So why would we even want to take our blinders off? Why move out of our discomfort zone? It may be endurance, but at least it's ours and we know how it works! This is a difficult question to address because leaving our discomfort zone means getting used to living in a world without walls, a world of infinite possibilities, and the guardian mind does not cope well with such freedom and expansiveness.

We may understand theoretically that the universe is more expansive than we can fathom. We may just be starting to realize, through quantum physics, that the distinctions among thought, energy, and matter are artificial. But these are concepts that the guardian mind cannot comprehend. The guardian was great when we were children, helping us learn limits that ensured our physical survival. Believing warnings such as "Look both ways before crossing the street" and "Don't take candy from strangers" protected us. But at some point in every tale, the child grows up, leaves home, and explores the world. The guardian self, scared of a larger world it cannot fully comprehend, becomes limited in its value to us. This is where our spirit must take over—and it longs to do so.

Our spirit, free thinker that it is, has never been interested in limitations. When we were children, our make-believe games engrossed us and felt real because we let our spirits play. As we mature, we look for meaning in life—through religion, nature, philosophy, therapy, books, art, or meditation. In some way, we all strive to drop our blinders and know more of the unknowable—that which is beyond our mind's grasp but calls to our spirit. Why else would we study the capacities of the human brain—its ability to imagine, to dream, to visualize and conceptualize? Why would we contemplate the existence of our soul, or the outer limits of the solar system? As terrified as our guardian may be to explore a life without limiting beliefs, the spirit longs to be free of restriction, find deeper meaning, and live in awe and wonder.

Many limiting beliefs, when shattered, cause fear at first. Just a few hundred years ago, people were terrified when the world was proven to be round, not flat. Galileo showed that Copernicus was right, that the earth was not the center of the universe but revolved around the sun. For this he was imprisoned. Such was the comfort of the familiar and the fear of questioning a belief.

It takes time for the guardian to let go of what is no longer true (or has never been true) and integrate something truer. The guardian requires help from the spirit to do so. The spirit has faith in possibilities, and even in the unknown. It gently coaxes the guardian out of the discomfort zone that doubles as a prison. The spirit says, "It's OK to step out of there. There is so much more for you over here. There is where you endure. Here is where you will be inspired. Drop your limiting beliefs, and come with me to explore the universe of possibilities."

🕐 Time In 🕐

Identify a limiting belief you hold about how life works that you would like to change. How would your life change if you discovered that something else was true?

The Ninety-Degree Turn
Toward the Extraordinary

If we want to explore this wider view, we can begin simply by seeing what futurist Buckminster Fuller called the *precessional effect*.

The precessional effect says that every action creates an often unknown or unnoticed benefit *just outside our awareness*. As an example, Fuller talks about how a bee seeks nectar by visiting flower after flower, not realizing that it is simultaneously performing the essential function of pollination. Like the bee, we may focus straight ahead, intent on what we're doing—our goals, our to-do lists, our chores—and miss the excitement or potential gifts available at just ninety-degree angles to either side of us.

The precessional effect suggests that by taking off our blinders—releasing our limiting beliefs—we find that we are in fact living in a much more complex, exciting, and unpredictable world than we may have believed.

We can choose to notice precessional effects in our daily lives. For example, if you are driving to the store during a rainstorm to get milk and you see a rainbow on the way, the precessional effect challenges you to pose the question, "Did I drive to the store to get milk, or to see the rainbow?" If you are stuck in a traffic jam on the way to work, the precessional effect invites you to ponder, "Perhaps this traffic jam is giving me the time I need to think about something. Or maybe it's keeping me from getting into an accident." "Did I stub my toe last week because I needed to slow down?" "Did I join the Sierra Club to see that awe-inspiring peak or to meet my partner?"

By expanding our perception, we can tickle our imagination, invite ourselves to get out of a rut, and unleash our creative capacity to thrive. Try it: just being aware of the concept of the precessional effect can create surprising results.

⏱ Time In ⏱

Today, take an item from your to-do list and apply the precessional effect. As you make the bed, fill the gas tank, run errands, or answer e-mail, ask yourself, "What else is around me right now that I would miss if I were not paying attention? What possible gift might there be in this experience?"

Time Jumping

Inevitably, we perceive others, the world, and ourselves through the filter of our judgments and beliefs. Just as surely, others perceive us through their own filter. Simply by remembering that we all have these filters, placed on us by our guardian to try to protect us from pain, we can decide not to react with knee-jerk quickness.

For example, when Jody's supervisor asked her to rewrite her report to include both an introduction and conclusion, he was trying to help this newcomer learn a better way to approach report writing. She, however, believed he meant, "You are doing a horrible job—you can't write, and I'm ready to fire you." Her guardian mind filtered his message instantly according to her past experience, trying to protect her from future humiliation by making her hypersensitive to criticism. The guardian says, "If I hear every criticism as a threat, perhaps I can avoid the inevitable." How could Jody see beyond her perception, which limited her capacity to take in all other relevant data?

First, she needed to slow down her reaction time. What did her supervisor actually say, as opposed to what she perceived? Many times we hear what we are prepared to hear and not what has been said. Have you ever played the game of telephone, where one person whispers a message in another person's ear, and then the message continues in this way from person to person? If so, then you know how rare it is for the message to end up intact by the time even four or five players have passed it along. One reason a message becomes distorted is that it is influenced by our perception.

Second, Jody needed to recognize her limiting beliefs. When she thought about this idea in my presence, she remembered being handed an F on a composition in high school, with no chance to redo her work. From that time on, she believed, "It's not fair. No one ever gives me a second chance. If I don't get it right the first time, I'm doomed." Inevitably, then, the F she received on that paper translated to being fired today.

Third, Jody needed to affirm a new thought that would free her from her limiting belief. She chose an affirmation: "I, Jody, am now becoming a competent writer." This not only encouraged her to practice the skills required but also allowed her to hear her supervisor's critique without filtering it through her negative belief, releasing her from endurance immediately.

Finally, she needed to get a reality check from her boss by asking open-ended questions: "How concerned are you about my work in general?" "How are you feeling about letting me have another stab at this report?" "Do you have more suggestions for me to help improve my writing skills?" All of these questions invited a truer reality, not further evidence for Jody's past limiting beliefs.

When we get angry or embarrassed or feel misunderstood or not good enough, we may misperceive reality and therefore time-jump, unknowingly, into our past. Usually, what we think upsets us is not really the source of our pain. Like Jody, we are often triggered by our past.

We cannot assume we will share the same perception as anyone else, or that our perception is correct. Perception, by definition, is neither correct nor incorrect. Perception implies that there is some-one perceiving reality through numerous filters: past experience, be-liefs, anxiety level, and education, as well as momentary physical, emotional, and spiritual states. The list of filters is as infinite as the possible number of perceptions.

Process for Change
Understanding Perception

Take a short walk with a friend, partner, or child. Stop and look at an object together. This can be a tree, a fence, a piece of paper on the ground, a cat—anything you agree to stop and notice. Then take turns saying, "What I see is _____. What I perceive is _____."

For example, if you are both focusing on a cat, one of you might say, "What I see is a cat sleeping on the fence. What I perceive is that it is lazy and enjoying the warmth of the sun." Your walking partner might say, "What I see is a black-and-white cat on the fence moving its ears. What I perceive is that it is pretending to sleep while it lis-tens for mice."

Practice this exercise with at least two more objects.

This process is designed to give you a direct experience of the dis-tinction between perception and reality. If two people can be walking together calmly and perceive the same object so differently, imagine how each of us perceives words from a past conversation, or a look on someone's face, or the tone of voice used in an argument. Imagine, then, how pervasive the influence of our limiting beliefs can be on our perception!

Throw Away Your Black-and-White Set

Any one of our limiting beliefs can hinder us from seeing the nuances of a situation or of another's motive. If we feel hurt or afraid of rejec-tion, we tend to perceive a situation in black and white only, as Jody did: "My boss criticized me. He wants to fire me." Most of us would deny that we oversimplify to such a degree, but in fact we often perceive our world in such a colorless fashion.

For the guardian self, the simpler the story, the better. This black-and-white perception protects us from confusion and further hurt. The guardian wants the world to make sense effortlessly: good guys versus bad guys, right versus wrong, perpetrator versus victim. The guardian tries to spare us from the vulnerable work of questioning our judgment, beliefs, and perception because if we question ourselves then we have to question our worldview. Once again, the guardian fears this. Our spirit, though, *wants* to question a worldview that keeps us in fear, pain, boredom, or hopelessness.

Our guardian also fears that if we question the validity of our perceptions—if we admit that we may be wrong—others will lose faith in us and then abandon us. To this end, our guardian may have us tell our skewed stories—the ones in which we are wearing the white hat—to anyone willing to hear and take our side. Once we roll out our side of the story, we are able to justify any and all of our behaviors, sounding like a five-year-old who argues, "Well, he punched me first. I had to hit him with my baseball bat." Black-and-white mentality tells us that either we let someone continue to hurt or anger us or we retaliate. It is the origin of revenge.

I am reminded of popular TV shows of the Judge Judy type, where the judge begins by asking for both sides of the story. Have you noticed how the stories are almost always so completely different that it is difficult to know whom to believe? Both parties invariably portray themselves (usually with a lot of attitude) as the innocent victim. To some extent, they have probably come to believe their own perception thanks to their guardian's belief that it has to be right or else. Once both parties' guardians have gained total control, no room is left for the truth. So a judge must decide, fairly or not, who wins and who loses. Often, *both* parties walk out of the courtroom feeling less than satisfied.

Perception that is based on fear and limiting beliefs causes us to lose our peripheral vision and make us color-blind. By letting our extraordinary spirit have an opportunity to calm our guardian, we can curb the drive to prove that we are right and that someone else is wrong, thereby resisting the urge to seek revenge for a real or imagined insult or hurt. We can get out of the courtroom and back into the classroom, where exploration—the work of the spirit—is the goal.

⏰   Time In   ⏰

As you go through your day today, pay attention to
where you may be seeing things from a black-and-white
perspective. Does holding this awareness cause you
to change your perception about a situation?

The Four Stages of Competency

You may need some practice in becoming aware of your limiting beliefs and black-and-white perceptions. It may take a while to stop believing them. Just recognizing them is an empowering first step.

Becoming competent in any activity—including recognizing and releasing limiting beliefs—is a process with four distinct and recognizable stages. Understanding at any given moment where we are in the process of becoming competent helps us if we feel frustrated and impatient with ourselves.

Remember when you learned to ride a bike or drive a car? When I first contemplated driving, I thought it would be fun. It looked easy enough when I saw others do it. However, when I got behind the wheel for the first time, I was humbled by the complexity of driving. How was I ever going to be able to remember to signal before a turn while putting my foot on the brake? How could other drivers talk or listen to the radio and drive at the same time? The choreography of driving seemed overwhelming, and I was sure that I would never master it.

The key, of course, was my willingness and motivation to practice. As I practiced, I became more coordinated in my efforts. When I finally started to feel competent, I patted myself on the back. After I had been driving for a while, I no longer needed to acknowledge myself for my driving skill. It simply became a habit.

We go through the same stages as we learn to question our perceptions and release our limiting beliefs. Let's look at the four stages of competency.

Stage One: Unconscious and Incompetent (Blinders on 24/7)

In stage one, we are both unconscious in our awareness and incompetent in our actions. In this first stage, we do not even recognize that there is a problem. In the realm of limiting beliefs and black-and-white perception, this is when we feel frustration, shame, hopelessness, or any other symptoms of endurance; but we don't know why. In stage one, we haven't yet questioned the authority of our thoughts and we take endurance for granted.

Congratulations; you're already past this stage.

Stage Two: Conscious and Incompetent (Peeking Around the Edges)

Stage two is often hard on the guardian self. In this stage, we start to recognize situations or patterns of behavior where we feel incompetent. Regarding perception and limiting beliefs, we begin to realize that we are stuck in a rut and want to do something about it but don't know where to begin. This is our first moment behind the wheel, and it can be frightening. We are hopeful that there is a light at the end of the tunnel but scared that we will never get out. Sometimes we try to go back to unconsciousness because we are afraid of the unfamiliar and of failing.

In stage two, we try to hang onto old behavior without fundamentally questioning our belief system, often exhausting ourselves in the process. The guardian self struggles for continued dominance, but we begin to notice the evidence against our old beliefs mounting. We still think that our limiting beliefs might be true, but we are willing to be wrong and let our frustration with endurance move us forward. We begin to peek around the edges of our blinders with new curiosity and courage.

Stage Three: Conscious and Competent
(Blinders off Most of the Time)

In stage three, we have taken off the blinders often enough that we no longer wish to put them back on. To become competent, we must now make a commitment to practicing new thoughts and behavior. Commitment, as motivational speaker and writer Zig Ziglar defines it, is about doing those things we said we would do long after the mood in which we said them has worn off. Our payoff for keeping our commitment to recognizing black-and-white perception and limiting beliefs is spontaneity and inspiration.

At first, competency occurs in fits and starts. We realize our detour into the territory of limiting beliefs only *after* we reach a dead end. Then, after practicing for a time, we begin to catch our mistakes *as* we make them.

With patience and time, we begin to recognize a limiting belief before we slip into old behavior and send ourselves back into endurance. At this point, we owe ourselves a pat on the back for our willingness to practice.

Stage Four: Unconscious and Competent
(Living Without Blinders)

In stage four, we no longer have to work so hard at changing our thoughts and finding evidence for new possibilities. We habitually question our own and others' limiting beliefs and perceptions. As a result, our life no longer feels boring and predictable. We feel an enthusiasm and curiosity about the world and see others and ourselves in a new light. We have new perspectives and wisdom to offer, and we feel of greater service to others. Life has become anything but ordinary.

Each of us must go through all four stages before we become naturals at recognizing our filters of perception and letting go of limiting beliefs. Remembering this helps us appreciate the sometimes difficult work of staying aware that our perceptions and limiting beliefs may blind us to the beauty of others, as well as to our own abilities. In stage four, our spirit reveals to us that we are much greater than any of our limiting beliefs, and so is everyone else.

🕐 Time In 🕐

Have you been able to see how you might gently relax your guardian's vigilance about your perceptions and limiting beliefs? Are you thinking about letting some of those limiting beliefs go? Which ones are you ready to release now?

❊ ❊

When we're stuck in endurance, we often long to break free but despair of ever being able to do so. Fortunately for us, our spirit is already free. It is not attached to being right about our perception or our limiting beliefs. So the question now becomes not so much how we can escape from the prison of our endurance but how to realize we already hold the key to our freedom.

Our guardian self has always had our best interest at heart. Yet its powerful voice at times convinces us that we prefer to be alone when we do not, that relationships are not trustworthy when this isn't true, or that the limitations we believe in are what God or the universe or life has chosen for us when actually there is a whole world out there just waiting for us. In return for the guardian's promises of safety, we are tempted to relinquish our spirit's longings.

In releasing our limiting beliefs (which the spirit never embraces anyway), we begin to see the truth of who we are. The world looks very different outside of the four gray walls of our endurance prison cell. Now we can stand in front of the mirror, quiet the voice of our guardian self for a moment, and begin to hear our spirit whispering, "See grace in your reflection."

Chapter Four

Drop Your Acts

Become Who You Already Are

And the day came when the risk to remain tight
in a bud was more painful than the risk it took to
blossom.

— *Anaïs Nin*

Throughout most of *Groundhog Day*, Phil had quite an act: the weathered, cynical guy who needed no one. It took living through a number of Groundhog Days for him to see that if only he dropped his act, people would respond to the real Phil very differently. We alternately cringe and cheer for Phil because we can identify; we expend a lot of energy trying to hide our self-judgment and fear from others by appearing as someone other than who we really are. We pretend to be more together than we feel, or we pretend not to care and hope that no one will see what we don't want them to see.

Lessons from *The Breakfast Club*

In another film, *The Breakfast Club*, five high school students are given detention on a Saturday. They are to remain in the school library all day with one assignment: to write a thousand-word essay describing who they think they are. But because this seems silly to most of them, they begin instead to try to figure out who the *others* are. At first they buy each other's act: the jock, the brain, the crazy one, the prom queen, the criminal. They cling to their own acts too, uncomfortably comfortable with their labels.

But as they are forced to spend many hours together, they become more authentic with each other, and the acts begin to fall away.

Each student starts to rebel against the restrictions of his or her image; as they do, their worlds are shaken, but they come to respect themselves and each other more. By the end of the day, they have decided to write only one essay among them, and it conveys the message that the adults in their lives see them only as they want to see them, in the most limited of ways, which is how they saw themselves before spending the day together. But what they learn is that each of them has attributes of the others within themselves. They are all capable of being smart, athletic, crazy, elitist, or rebellious.

The Breakfast Club movingly depicts the process of discovering who we are beneath our act. The students, hiding behind their roles, initially brutalize each other verbally with their judgments. But the moment each student reveals more of who he or she is, they all can see the illusion of their judgment and are released from their fear of one another. They leave detention as comrades, with dignity and wisdom: the judgments were real, but they are not true.

We take our cue from our guardian self when we put on the armor of an act. In it, we behave incongruently with what we really feel. When in an act, we sacrifice our authenticity for protection. The labels we pick and choose for ourselves are designed to protect us from hurt. Or to ensure that everyone will love us. Or to garner respect we are afraid we don't really deserve. Or . . . the list of fears fueling our acts is infinite. The problem is that after we have our act for so long we cannot remember who we are without it.

⏱ Time In ⏱

In what situations do you feel you have to put on an act?
What do you fear will happen if you are your true self
in such a situation?

The Sour-Grapes Act

Hank, an amicable man who worked as a corporate executive, felt rejected when Benjamin, his coworker, stopped asking him to play golf on Saturdays. When Hank overheard Benjamin laughing and talking to another coworker about *their* last round of golf together, Hank told himself that he didn't enjoy Benjamin's company that much anyway—really, he preferred golfing alone.

Hank and I talked about how he was using a sour-grapes act to try to protect himself from feeling rejected. This strategy comes, of course, from the famous fable by Aesop, in which a fox declares that he doesn't care that he can't reach an attractive bunch of grapes because he imagines they are probably sour anyway.

As long as Hank denied that he liked Benjamin, he was stuck feeling rejected. In fact, he obsessively tried to figure out what he did wrong and why Benjamin didn't like him. Hank's fear-based thinking deafened him to the one voice that could truly help him: the voice of his spirit.

Hank's sour-grapes act did not really spare him from enduring fear hurt, or rejection. Shortly after Hank and I talked about the courage required to face his fear, he decided to ask Benjamin directly why they hadn't played golf together lately. Benjamin replied, "Look, I'm competitive enough at work. When I get out on the golf course, I like to relax. On the other hand, you like to bet on every hole. It's nothing personal, Hank. I just don't think our styles mesh on the course."

Hank had assumed that Benjamin would be just as driven at golf as he was in the boardroom. Now he understood why he had been rejected. "Benjamin, I don't need to play competitively with you. I'd actually *like* to relax and enjoy the game. Give me another chance," he smiled, "and I promise: no more side bets." The next week, Benjamin and Hank played a friendly game of golf and went back to having a weekly date.

Benjamin's rejection of Hank was real, but the reason for it was not what Hank imagined. By dropping his sour-grapes act, Hank was able to discover the truth and repair their relationship.

In our attempt to ward off any possibility of abandonment, we often spurn others before they can abandon us, pretend we don't care, cheat and lie to keep others near, or become a victim so that others will pity us even if they don't love us. To perform these duties, we must don a mask—otherwise, we would too easily recognize our own trickery.

⏱ Time In ⏱

Think of a situation in which your fear of abandonment
or rejection affected your behavior. What act did you
use to get you through the situation? How would
you have behaved if you had been authentic?

The Victim Act

Howard, a physician with a practice in general medicine, looked more like a professional athlete than a doctor. For the past two years, he had come home every night complaining to his wife, Marty, about insurance paperwork, the HMOs controlling his practice, pharmaceutical salespeople hyping drugs, and lazy employees. He was generally irritable and cranky. One night, Marty had heard enough of his complaints and spoke up: "I don't believe any of it anymore."

"What do you mean? It's all true. It's not my fault that medicine has changed so much since I first started my practice."

"It may all be true, but you aren't unhappy and frustrated because of your long list of complaints. You're miserable for some other reason. Find out what it is, because I don't want to hear your whining anymore. I miss my husband, and I want him back."

Howard felt smacked by a two-by-four. He was tempted to grumble something in retaliation, but he knew Marty was right. So he came to a session with me ready to figure out why he felt like such a victim of his profession. He started with, "I love my patients, but I'm miserable every day."

"What would you rather be doing?"

"I'd rather be practicing sports medicine. But I have a mortgage and two kids to get through college, so that's out. I would have to decrease my clinical hours to have time to get certified in this specialty, and I just can't see how to do it."

"Have you brainstormed this with Marty?"

"I have no business asking anything of her. She gave up her practice as an orthopedic surgeon when our first son started high school. We felt he needed some guidance at a critical time of his life."

"So she doesn't even know what you really want? My guess is that you feel guilty about Marty giving up her practice, so now you think you can't ask her for anything else. In a way, you're trying to protect yourself from the risk that Marty might reject you. But by playing the victim, guess what? Marty is rejecting you anyway because she's tired of your complaints."

This argument was irrefutable to Howard. He wanted Marty to read between the lines and figure out that she could help him realize his dream of switching to sports medicine—without having to spell it out for her. "That's exactly what we do when we're in victim thinking, Howard. We try to get people to come to our rescue without having to ask, so that we can avoid rejection or abandonment. But then people get tired of our whining. So we may as well ask for what we really want."

Howard recognized a familiar pattern in this setup with Marty. As a child, he felt humiliated for wanting things, whether it was a bicycle or a book—after all, as he was so often reminded, children were starving in China. As a result, he learned to become indirect and only hint about what he wanted. Sometimes this worked, sparing him the guilt of believing he was too selfish.

When Howard finally told Marty the truth, she laughed in relief. "OK," she said with surprising ease. "You can work part-time and we'll sell this house and downsize. I'd rather have a happy husband than a big alimony check and an empty house."

Howard had been manifesting his limiting beliefs, not his spiritual longings. To tune into his dreams and create a life, not just a living, Howard needed to see the futility and damage of playing the victim to avoid rejection. In the end, the trade-off of a smaller house for a happier life was worthwhile.

The consequences of playing the victim role are severe. Our self-esteem continues to diminish as our sense of hopelessness and helplessness increases. So, why would we play this role if it is so harmful to our spirit? In addition to trying to head off feeling rejected or humiliated, we may don the role of victim if we were victimized as children.

Children who are routinely abused or humiliated tend to confuse love with emotional pain and unwittingly continue to attract abuse into their lives. Our guardian self always feels that we will be safer recreating the familiar, including our own victim role, no matter how painful. So instead of shunning abuse we may subconsciously lure it to us. We embrace the victim role again and again, not because we enjoy it but because it feels normal. *We must remember that we are always creating our reality from our thoughts.* That's why every painful situation as an adult, every experience of repeated Groundhog Days, offers an opportunity to examine and change our thoughts to heal our wounds.

Our spirit isn't going anywhere; it's at least as tenacious as our guardian self. Even better, it is always looking for a way to heal pain, not just avoid it. Whenever we get into a pattern, such as becoming a victim, the spirit sees this as an opportunity for healing. It gives us messages, if we listen. It works on our behalf, if we let it. With its inspiration, we can break free and thrive.

The Competency Act

The flip side of the victim act is the competency act. This is quite popular because the short-term gains conceal the long-term losses.

Carla described herself as "a smart cookie," but she had to quit high school at sixteen to help support her family. Now, in her late twenties, she was determined to work at more than just a dead-end job that paid minimum wage. But rather than get credentialed or certified, she decided she was smart enough to fool employers. So whenever she filled out an employment application, she would lie about her education, claiming to have a bachelor's degree. This was her justification: "I have more qualifications for that job than any other applicant who has a four-year degree. So why should I blow my chances of getting the job? I deserve it. There's no harm in lying. In fact, I'm doing them a favor because they're getting the best candidate for the job—me."

I wanted to jump in and give her a morality lecture. But who was I to judge her? Could I claim never to have practiced embellishment? How many of us can say we have never spiced up a resume by enhancing a job title? Who hasn't claimed achievements that weren't solely ours, stretched dates to cover employment gaps, or let an employer assume graduation by posting college attendance dates?

Most of us have experience in this competency act. Carla simply became a master at justifying it. But what drove her—what drives all of us when we pretend to be better than what we think we are—is fear of failure, loss, or abandonment.

I could not tell Carla what the consequences of her deception would be in the future. But I knew that, as surely as if I had a crystal ball in front of me, her spirit must already be suffering the consequences of being dominated by her protective guardian.

"Carla, when you lie about your education and then get hired, how do you feel with your colleagues?"

"At first I feel brilliant, but after a while I end up feeling like I'm trying to prove myself, and like I have to be on my toes so they don't figure it out."

"So you don't ever really feel equal to them?"

"I *do* feel equal. I just don't think they'll believe I'm equal if they find out the truth."

"Carla, you're projecting your self-judgment onto other people. I have a hard time believing you when you say you feel equal. What do you feel about not having graduated from high school or college?"

"I wish I had been able to continue my education, but I couldn't afford it when I was younger. Now I'm too old."

"Is that your judgment? That's hard to buy. Many people go back to school to complete a degree. There are many online colleges and evening programs designed for those who have already experienced the work world. What are you really afraid of?"

"I don't know. Maybe I'm afraid I'll flunk."

"If you never test this, you'll be condemning yourself to feeling less than others for the rest of your life. That seems like a prison sentence you don't deserve."

"I just don't know if I can do it. I want to give you a hundred excuses right now, but I know you won't believe any of them."

"Will you?"

"Oh, I could probably convince myself. Remember, I'm the master of justifications."

Carla didn't come back for any more coaching, so I don't know if she ever took the risk of signing up for high school or college courses. I hope she did, so that she could stop enduring in the prison of her competency act and enjoy true camaraderie at work.

Ken's situation was quite different, but his competency act took its toll. Just before he began seeing me, he had an important meeting with his staff about the merger of his company with a much larger one. He played the role of the competent manager who had a handle on everything, even though he was afraid of the chaos that the merger would bring. During the meeting, he sat with his arms folded, nodding his head, asking questions so that he would avoid the hot seat of being asked anything he couldn't answer.

Ken could barely concentrate on the meeting because he was worried that his act was transparent and that people would think he was a phony. Even more disconcerting, he felt as though he was not the only one in the room doing it. Reflecting on the meeting later, he told me, "I'm pretty sure that everyone else was just as scared as I was. I think some important topics never got addressed because we were all too afraid to broach them."

In hindsight, Ken thought that if he had been authentic by sharing his own concerns about the merger, he would have helped others open up to talk about their own fears. He decided then and there that it was time to drop his competency act, so he called a second meeting. When he then came back to see me, he was obviously proud: "I told everyone that I thought we probably all had some anxiety about the merger. I put my fears on the table and encouraged everyone else to do the same. Instead of pretending that I had all the answers, I asked the group to help each other work through some of the problems. Everyone was relieved to be able to be truthful, but no one more than me."

The Integrity Act

By all accounts, at least outwardly, Paul had it all. Until a few years ago, he had a beautiful wife and a daughter with whom he shared what looked like the perfect life. They traveled around the world and hobnobbed with celebrities and socialites.

One day, his wife Lilly found a hotel receipt as she was emptying Paul's shirt pocket before throwing it into the laundry pile. Now, finding hotel receipts in his pockets was not unusual. He had hundreds of them from his business travels and their personal trips. What was strange about this receipt is that it was for a hotel in Atlanta—and they lived in Atlanta. Why would he need to go to a hotel in their home town? She could think of only one answer, so she confronted him that night.

Paul admitted he was having an affair. In fact, with very little prodding, he was willing to admit to several affairs. She was devastated and insisted they get counseling. He agreed. But when they came to a session, he stated, without a trace of irony in his voice, "I may have had affairs, but I'm a man of integrity. It was just a mistake. Lilly needs to let it go so we can move on in our lives." He was angry and impatient with her feelings of hurt and betrayal.

I suspect that Paul's man-of-integrity stance was an act to mask his fear of abandonment. His protective guardian was probably advising him to trade reality for myth, to try to help him argue his way back into Lilly's heart, but as long as he kept his stance, he could not heal; nor could she trust him. Still, he held onto his act for dear life— and they divorced within a year. To this day, he believes that the failure in the marriage is all her burden to carry. He does not understand why she would not forgive, trust, and love him again. He contends to anyone who will listen that he is the victim of her stubbornness and punitive nature.

We can all let our fear masquerade as pride and then present ourselves to others (and even ourselves) as more virtuous than we actually are. Our fear of abandonment can be so pervasive that we refuse to question our own perception. Like Paul, we can paint ourselves into a corner and then blame the company that manufactured the paint.

🕐   Time In   🕐

In what situation have you tried to look better on the
outside than you were feeling about yourself inside?
How did the situation play out? If you had been authentic,
what other outcome might have been possible?

The Good-Girl/Good-Guy Act

The good-girl act is one I know all too well. At the age of nineteen, after a painful "affair" (which you will read about later), I wanted to create a new image. I left home to attend a university in another city and moved into the dormitory. No one knew me there, so my plan could be executed perfectly. I began to dress very conservatively and behave with a naïveté that belied the sixties' counterculture milieu of my upbringing in San Francisco, as well as my sexual history. Soon after arriving at my new school, I met a twenty-three-year-old Mormon man who was innocent and naïve.

I latched onto him and didn't let go until he asked me to marry him. On our wedding day, I wore no makeup, had my hair cropped short and plain, and wore what can best be described as the "poofiest" dress since poodle skirts went out of style. I have absolutely no memory of the ceremony except that my jaw hurt so badly from tension that I could not utter my *I dos* without feeling excruciating pain. Coincidentally (or not), I also got stung by a bee during the reception. My leg swelled to elephantiasis proportions, with itching that lasted for weeks.

The persuasive voice of my protective guardian convinced me to stay safe in my role of the good girl (aka loving wife) for the next two years, although I experienced worsening jaw pain. My husband became more and more depressed during this time, to the point that he no longer showered or dressed. I behaved as though I felt kindness and compassion, although most of the time I resented him. My husband suffered for my good-girl act: he felt my judgment, regardless of how much I tried to hide or deny it. He became more isolated in his depression, and I began to feel just a tad crazy.

Pain is often the motivator to get our butt in gear and start healing. One day I walked into the Women's Center on campus and asked for the first available appointment with a counselor. In just a few sessions, she helped me get out of my act by encouraging me to be truthful with my husband. I felt frightened of what I was discovering to be my truth, but my "lockjaw"—my unconscious lock on my medium of communication—would not let me ignore my painful situation any longer. Besides, watching my husband sink into deeper depression was more frightening than having a heart-to-heart talk, regardless of the consequences.

I told my husband that although I cared about him I had never been in love with him. I acknowledged that I had married him for all the wrong reasons and that I was sorry for having done so. He felt sad and hurt, but he was also relieved. He admitted that trying to be a good husband when he was depressed felt like too much pressure.

We were coconspirators, and it was time to end our hollow marriage. Had I not done so, I'm pretty sure my body's symptoms and ailments would have escalated along with his depression. As Dr. Christiane Northrop points out, if we ignore the source of our suffering our body will eventually present its bill. Our bodies were exacting pretty stiff payments. When presented with our bill for enduring fear, self-judgment, limiting beliefs, and acts, we paid up and moved on.

Using our act to get what we think we want backfires because the act becomes a trap. Once our act is established, others may expect us to keep performing it at all times. We become resentful from the pressure we then feel to maintain the act, and we come to believe that we cannot be loved for who we really are.

The Mellow Act

Sean had a ponytail and a sauntering gait. Women rejected him, he told me, even though he worked hard at his easygoing image. When I asked him why he thought he had to present himself to women this way, he looked at me as though I were dense. He slowly drew out the words he spoke next: "Because that's what women *want.*" The *t* on *want* punctuated his sarcasm.

"Well, it's clear right off the bat that mellow is not what you are, are you?"

"No," he replied with a shake of the head, "and that's what scares women away. I'm too intense, apparently."

"I'm not sure that intensity is your problem. But you do seem angry about your state of affairs. Where did you first hear that you were too intense?" The word *too* was, for me, the tip-off that Sean was judging himself.

"My dad once told me that I was so intense that no woman would ever want to marry me."

"Now, that's a pretty intense statement, and damning as well. Maybe your dad ignored something you were angry about and accused you of being too intense instead."

Sean thought about this and decided it rang true. Whenever he was angry, his father would put him down. So Sean thought that if he acted as though nothing bothered him, his father wouldn't have anything to use against him. Since the opposite of intense seemed to be mellow, he went for it. With women, Sean dressed the part and used the language of mellowspeak, but inevitably his intensity would pop through and that was the end of the relationship.

Here's the really interesting part: Sean didn't respect the women who were attracted to his act. "I'm sick of women who can't handle a strong and committed man, who run with their tail between their legs whenever I say 'boo.'"

Sean had created a vicious cycle, trying to attract women by acting mellow, yet disliking the women he drew to him with this act. The key, clearly, was for him to respect who he really was so that he would find a partner whom he could respect as well. When he finally saw this, he decided to do something about it.

He started with an affirmation that countered his father's ridiculous prophecy: "I, Sean, with all my intensity and passion, am creating a dynamic relationship with a woman I love and admire."

Sean went at affirming his true nature with what turned out to be characteristic energy. The next time I saw him, he had cut his hair, dropped both his mellow language and his sarcasm, and walked with purpose in his step. Now a very different kind of woman was drawn into his orbit, and soon he met Fay, who was challenged and attracted by his fiery energy. Eventually they married, and they have now shared a life for many years. She considers his intensity a gift that contributes to her own passions. When they had their first child, he wrote me a note saying, "We've got one like me. He never sleeps, feels all his emotions very strongly, and is high maintenance. We're thrilled!"

Sean didn't just drop his act; he fired the director, burned the whole script, and wrote a new play. That is empowerment. That is the spirit set free. He serves as an inspiration to never judge who we are or settle for the dreariness of endurance.

Burn Your Old Script

There are as many acts as there are people to create them. If not the victim act, the competent act, the good-girl/good-guy act, or the mellow act, then another act will do. Depending on our fears, our personality, our family dynamics, and even our culture, we may have learned the stoic act, the happy-go-lucky act, or the inscrutable act. We may even have cultivated a spiritual act, creating a façade of righteousness or serenity.

Have you ever acted the role of the class clown? the hero? the martyr, or the intellectual, or the rescuer? Have you been the loner, the loser, the perfect friend, the loving partner? Of course, we may truthfully *be* funny, witty, confident, competent, helpful, loving, spiritual, or shy. But we are not *always* anything. These personality traits and behaviors become an act when we use them to protect ourselves, sacrificing our deeper truth in service of fear-based beliefs.

We can replace our act with the joyful permission to *become more of who we really are*. We are limitless in our choice of new behaviors in the process of this discovery. Phil finally learned this lesson in *Groundhog Day*. Once he was willing to drop his cynical act and discovered the joy of being vulnerable and authentic, he became more loving and tender than he had ever imagined himself to be.

❀ ❀

We are all more than who we have imagined ourselves to be. Becoming familiar with our inner cast of characters helps us find our authentic spirit, which knows that who we really are is much more interesting than any character we could possibly play.

Chapter Five

Break the Spell of Fear

Make Fear Your Ally

You gain strength, courage, and confidence by
every experience in which you really stop to look
fear in the face. You must do the thing which you
think you cannot do.

—*Eleanor Roosevelt*

Before Juan even sat down, he announced that he was here for just
one session. "I don't really have any big problems. I don't even know
why I'm here. My friend Mel—you know, your client?—told me I
should make an appointment." He looked slightly bored with the
whole idea of being in my office.

"Well, do you have any small problems you were discussing with
Mel that would make him think seeing me was a good idea?"

"I don't know; I'm confused." He paused. Endurance in the form
of confusion is often the first symptom that fear has us under its spell.
It was true for Juan.

"I have one small problem, I guess. I've had this girlfriend for
five years. She wants to get married and have a child. I was married
before and have a teenage son. I'm not sure I want to do this again."

"Which *this* are you unsure about: marriage or a child?" I expected
him to say *child*, but he surprised me.

"Oh, I'd love to have another child. I love my son, but he's becoming more independent now. I'm still young enough to have another child, and I have more time to devote to a child now than I
did before. It's the commitment to my girlfriend that I'm confused
about."

"Can you tell me more about your feelings for her?"

"She's great, really. She's the most unconditionally loving, patient woman I've ever known. Why she stays with me I don't know."

"Why? What have you done?"

He looked puzzled. "What do you mean?"

"You just said that you didn't know why she stays with you. Have you done something to deserve being abandoned by her?"

The blasé look dropped right off his face and Juan stared back at me with that deer-in-the-headlights look. "Whoa, that was fast. I thought I'd get to tiptoe around this for a while. All right, there is something I've done. But she doesn't know about it."

"So it's a secret."

"Yes. I'll tell you, since I'm here and we've gotten this far. But don't try to convince me to confess it to her. It won't happen."

"It's your choice. But before you tell me, I want to tell you about a belief that I have so you know more about me. I believe that our secrets run the show. I believe that if you have a secret you feel guilty about, you will remain confused about your feelings because guilt creates separation from ourselves and from others. I don't claim to have a crystal ball, but I will tell you that, from my experience, you cannot have true intimacy and a guilty secret simultaneously."

"Wait. You're saying it's my secret that's keeping me confused about marrying my girlfriend?"

"I'd bet on it. I would also bet that you aren't so happy with the person you look at in the mirror every morning. If you don't think you deserve her love, it's going to be hard to let it in."

"Great. Then you're telling me that there's no way out of this. I may as well just go back and break up with her."

"Either that or tell her your big secret."

"I can't. It would hurt her too much."

"Juan, you can't tell me that you're keeping this secret for her sake. If you were worried about her feelings, you probably wouldn't have done whatever you did to begin with. Aren't you really more afraid that she'll abandon you?"

The Creative Logic of Fear

Guilt is an indicator that we have a conscience, but when we feel guilty about something our response is sometimes anything but altruistic. Because feeling guilty triggers our belief that we are unworthy, our protective guardian can take control and dress up our guilt with loftier motives than we really hold. Juan was trying to keep up his image of being OK—a good guy who just wanted to protect his girlfriend from being hurt—because he was afraid of facing his worst fear about himself: that he was unworthy of love. This fear was driving his decision to reject rather than be rejected.

"Juan, if you keep your secret and go home and break up with her, she's gone from your life anyway. The outcome is the same as what you're afraid of. And you still won't like the guy in the mirror, right?"

His protective guardian was nothing if not tenacious. "If I break up with her, I can start fresh with someone else—you know, a clean slate. Besides, I told you that I don't know that I really love her." He was starting to squirm in his chair.

"Juan, you can break up with her without ever confessing your guilty secret. You can go on to the next woman and never do to her what you did to this woman, whatever it is. But how much love will you ever feel you deserve if you don't clean this up?"

"Maybe I just won't be in another close relationship," he shrugged. "I can have casual girlfriends and go out and have fun."

"Then what about your longing for another child? What about your obvious attraction to this kind, unconditionally loving woman? By the way, if you think she's unconditional with her love, why are you so afraid she's going to leave you?"

"Because what I did was really bad. She'd be a fool to stay with me."

"So when are you going to tell me what you did?" I waited.

He took a deep breath, looked at his feet, and said quietly, "OK, I cheated on her." After a pause, he added, "more than once." His affairs had occurred before he and his girlfriend made a commitment to monogamy, but he felt guilty because he knew that she assumed he was faithful to her, and he had never let on that her assumption was not valid.

"Juan, you realize that in holding this secret and possibly breaking up with her you are deciding her fate too, not just your own. By controlling the flow of information—by not telling her your reasons for leaving—you're probably going to leave her very confused. Even if you don't love her, does she deserve to remain in the dark about why you are breaking up with her? You already disrespected her by being with other women. Isn't withholding the truth even more disrespectful? Maybe your fear of being abandoned has been so big that you're letting this fear decide everything for you."

He was still looking down at his feet.

"Juan," I asked more gently, "what happened in your marriage?"

"Do you mean, did I cheat on my wife? Yes, I did."

"And did you feel guilty?"

"Of course."

"Did you stop having loving feelings for her?"

"Yes. I divorced her because I felt nothing for her anymore. I mean, I liked her very much, but I had lost any loving feelings."

"OK, I think we have a pattern here, don't you? You have affairs, you feel bad, your guilt disconnects you from any other feelings, and then you abandon before you can be abandoned."

Juan was nodding sadly in agreement. "When you put it like that, it seems so stupid. Can't I just complete the loop here one more time and start fresh? Or maybe I'll just marry my girlfriend. I don't have to know if I love her. She's a great person and she loves me. I'll be a good husband and father. Isn't that good enough?"

A Slippery Slope

Of course, he was free to make his own choices. But he wasn't really free so long as fear was fueling his choices. We hadn't even gotten to the self-judgment and limiting beliefs that triggered his deception.

"Juan, here's what I think—especially if you're serious about wanting only one session. If you don't break your pattern now, and if you do marry your girlfriend, you'll remain ambivalent about the relationship. It will eventually lose momentum and stagnate, and you'll get bored or have another affair, and eventually you'll break up. If you don't think you deserve her love, what else could you do?"

"You're telling me I'm trapped."

"I'm telling you that your fear of being abandoned is making you *think* you're trapped. And your self-judgment that you are unworthy is ruining your relationships, one by one. What you are on is a slippery slope."

He sat quietly for a few minutes. "I need to think about all this. I can't believe I'm actually considering confessing. I'm not promising you anything."

He walked out of my office afraid, but he was a lot less confused about the decision he needed to make. I wondered if I would ever hear from one-session Juan again.

To my surprise, he called me five days later. I could hear his relief over the phone. He had told his girlfriend the truth. She did not suspect infidelity, but she told him that she knew something was bothering him because every time they had a close, intimate evening he would pull away. His confession triggered her hurt from past betrayals, and she was shaken. She told him that she would stay with him, and that she really did appreciate his honesty—in her experience, men usually said "I'll call you" and never showed up again. But she wanted six months to reassess their relationship. Juan was floored that she didn't abandon him on the spot.

"So how do you feel about her right now?" I asked.

"I love her very much," he said with emotion. "I don't feel confused at all. I do feel bad about hurting her, but I want to understand my limiting beliefs, as you call them. And she wants to grow from this too. Five days ago I didn't even know that I had a right to hope for anything. Today, I pray that we can make it through this."

They did. A year after the first session, bolstered by some further insight about the sources of his limiting beliefs and self-judgment, they were married. I was honored to be their minister. They are now the parents of twin girls.

How Fear, Secrets, and Lies Are Intertwined

When Juan first came to see me, he was tortured by indecision, yet his first impulse was to endure with his secret because he feared what would happen if he told the truth. This is how fears, secrets, and lies are intertwined. If you think about any lie you have ever told or any secret you have withheld, you will probably recognize that fear motivated the impulse. If we had no fear, we would have no reason to lie or withhold the truth. But our fears often override our commitment to integrity or courage. Even though lying causes us to lose self-esteem and feel powerless, fear convinces us that the consequences of truth are more dire than our current suffering.

By our very human nature, we fear loneliness, ridicule, rejection, and death. Even if we can't articulate our fear at a given moment, we know its telltale signs: the heart pounds, the mind races, we want to lock ourselves away in safety or run at the first hint of danger. Fear's function is to signal danger. If the fear switch is always on, however, it will constrict us physically, emotionally, and spiritually, keeping us in endurance. *But we are not simply the sum total of our fears.*

Giving fear all the power keeps us mired in confusion, afraid to move or make a mistake. When fear narrows our capacity to see the rich beauty of what is real and what is possible, it's past time to turn around, stare fear in the face, and say "No, not this time."

⏲ Time In ⏲

Are you feeling confused about making the right
decision on an issue? What fears may be clouding
your mind? What do your fears tell you to do?
Can you hear your spirit at all? What does
your spirit have to say about this issue?

Running from a Past That Is Running You

As Colin discovered, the secrets we keep can end up running our lives in a way we never anticipated. Colin lived what appeared to be a very ascetic life, working in a bookstore, eating only vegetarian foods, and riding a bicycle rather than driving a car whenever possible. He tried hard not to be a conspicuous consumer, and he meditated twice a day for an hour at each sitting. Yet he found himself frustrated with his "lack of progress." At thirty-one years old, he thought he should feel more peaceful; instead, he felt isolated and restless, participating in online chat rooms for three hours every night.

I asked him if anything from his past was bothering him. "What's the difference?" he said calmly. "The past is the past."

When I suggested that the past might be responsible for his current frustration, Colin reluctantly gave in and shared the old scene that his mind replayed endlessly. At fifteen, he was asked to baby-sit a neighbor's two-year-old daughter. Colin had no interest in baby-sitting and felt resentful, but he agreed to do it after his parents pressured him to help the neighbors out this one time. The little girl missed her parents, didn't really know Colin, and cried most of the evening. Colin didn't have a clue how to calm her down. Worse, he was afraid that she would make herself sick from crying and that her parents would think he had done a terrible job.

Finally, he became so frustrated with her incessant screaming that he shook her. Stunned, she cried even more loudly. Finally, she cried herself to sleep. When her parents came home, Colin lied and said that they had played together and that everything was fine.

Once home that night, remorseful and frightened of his own anger and of being found out, Colin decided that he was terrible with children and would never have any of his own. He also decided that he would live within a highly controlled environment so that his anger would never harm anyone again.

After Colin finished telling his story, he was flooded with shame and remorse and broke down in tears. It was clear to him now that he had deluded himself by thinking he could experience peace while carrying around feelings of guilt and remorse. He hoped that he could just make these feelings go away by being "good" now. But he was being run by his past as he was running from it. With sudden clarity, he knew that it was time to tell the truth.

He felt compelled to call the parents of this girl (who now attended college). When he told them about that night, they said they knew that something happened because their daughter was very quiet and withdrawn the next morning. Colin apologized to them and asked if they would give him their daughter's phone number so he could also apologize to her.

Colin called her and identified himself, expecting her to react with anger; instead, she seemed neutral but curious. He asked her if she remembered that he once babysat her. She did not. Colin could not believe she did not remember that night; he had thought of it with horror every day for years. Colin told her what he had done to her and said that he was sorry he had frightened her. She responded with sympathy and told him that she hoped he could now forgive himself. Just because she did not remember him shaking her did not mean that Colin felt relief. He believed that she might have gone on to make unconscious decisions about men, just as he had apparently made unconscious decisions about himself. Nonetheless, he was grateful for her forgiveness.

Colin made so many decisions and endured so much pain because of a long-held secret. Although he had always thought that he shunned light-hearted fun and hedonism for valid political and social reasons, it was his relentless self-judgment tamping down all the joy in his life. Once Colin took the risk to reveal his guilty secret, he could begin to feel compassion for the fifteen-year-old boy he once was, clueless about child development and resentful about being pressured into doing something he felt unprepared to do. His spiritual practice deepened, and his isolation diminished after speaking his truth.

⏲   Time In   ⏲

In what situation are you currently lying or keeping a guilty secret? What is the worst-case scenario you have imagined arising from telling the truth? What are the consequences you have been paying for holding onto your secret or lie? How would you feel about yourself if you told your truth?

The Ultimate Endurance and Its Origin

The ultimate endurance is to fear that we are unworthy of love and then to behave in a way that proves to ourselves that this is true. Juan and Colin were both hurtful to others or to themselves, not because they were fundamentally unworthy of love but because each of these men *believed* they were unworthy of love.

Rather than face his fear that he was unworthy of love, Juan's survival strategy was to leave before he got left, which allowed him to believe that he was being left for being a cheater, not for being inherently unworthy. This creative logic helped him avoid his deeper self-judgment, but he was making a mess of his life.

Sounds self-destructive, doesn't it? But I'm willing to bet that it also has an all-too-familiar ring. Each one of us has had experiences that led us to question our fundamental value as a human being. No human being has been exempted from the pain of being rejected, ridiculed, criticized, shamed, or abandoned at one time or another. If we have lived at all, we have allowed our guardian self to help us avoid the painful self-judgment that we are unworthy while behaving in a way that reflects this underlying belief.

Our strategies vary. We may try to avoid this pain by rejecting others before they reject us, as Juan did. Or we may become aloof and protective of our heart, as Colin did. We may become vigilant in our suspicions and act belligerent or angry, pushing love away before it gets close enough to hurt us.

If we fundamentally believe the self-judgment that we are not worthy, we will go out of our way to gather evidence to support this illusion, creating situation after situation to validate our unworthiness. We don't do this because we enjoy endurance; we do this because fear has us under its spell.

When we are under fear's spell, we let our protective guardian make decisions without consulting our spirit. These decisions to lie and hold guilty secrets are the guardian's feeble attempts to avoid our self-judgment of unworthiness and our fear of abandonment. Even though this strategy has never worked to bolster our self-esteem and never will, the guardian struggles, believing that maybe this time we will be spared.

In our fear of abandonment, we often become increasingly needy—demanding that others give us more love, more attention, or more respect to make up for what we cannot give ourselves. Or, if we have no one else who will put up with our neediness, we may demand more stuff in our lives—nicer clothes, a newer car, a more expensive home, or a raise. In this driven state, how can we possibly break fear's spell?

First of all, we cannot heal what we ignore. Acknowledging that we are afraid is a good start because it puts us on the path from unconscious incompetence (stage one of the four stages of competence) toward conscious competence. We must admit that if we are in endurance, fear must be keeping us there. If you recognized one of your strategies in the preceding paragraph, your spirit has just whispered to you. It is asking you to pay attention to fear, not avoid it.

⏱ Time In ⏱

Think of a situation where you were demanding.
Maybe you told someone that you *needed* something rather
than stating that you *wanted* something. What were you
afraid of if the person did not give you what you supposedly
needed? On a scale of one to ten, how worthy were
you feeling when you demanded whatever it was?

Living Through Your Worst-Case Scenario

As a seminar leader, I taught public speaking courses for more than twenty years to employees in government, the private sector, and nonprofit organizations. Most participants took the course not to improve their speaking skills per se but to overcome their intense fear of public speaking. In a survey conducted by Schacter and McCauley, speaking in front of an audience was ranked as Americans' number one fear—above the fear of death (perhaps because we believe we will have to face public speaking sooner).

To address participants' fears head-on, I gave them the assignment of exaggerating their fear. I asked them to pretend they had made the worst blunder they could make in front of their audience. Then they were to imagine everyone pointing at them and laughing in their face. I asked them to feel as much humiliation as they could muster while imagining this worst-case scenario. It didn't take much for them to feel humiliated since this was the fear with which they walked into class.

Then I asked, "And now what? So it has happened. Your worst public speaking nightmare has just been realized. What do you do now?"

Participants inevitably found that once they quit trying to avoid their fear and actually imagined living through their dreaded nightmare, the fear dissipated and the humiliation waned. They quickly came to feel proud that they had made the courageous choice to speak, regardless of the outcome. Because they made a decision based on feeling good about themselves, the responses of others no longer mattered as much.

The minute you stop running or hiding from fear, something amazing happens. As you turn around to face your fear head on, the spell is broken. If you have ever entered a competition—a swim meet, a spelling bee, a debate—you've faced down fear. If you have ever gotten up the nerve to speak out against an injustice—perhaps with your child's teacher over an unfair grade, or with a boss who overlooked you for a promotion, or about a moving violation you didn't deserve—you've faced down fear. Regardless of the outcome—win or lose, yelled at or praised—you most likely felt more self-respect and dignity because you made the choice to face your fears courageously, thus making fear your ally.

⏰ Time In ⏰

Think about a situation in which you chose courage over fear. What happened? How did you feel inside?

Some fears are easier to face than others. Sometimes, it takes numerous attempts before fear's spell is completely broken. I found that it took many years to break the spell of fear about something that affected me deeply as a child. This is the story I promised you in the preceding chapter, the reason I ended up as the confused, poofy-dressed bride of a man I wasn't in love with.

When I was eleven years old, a new couple moved in across the street. They were very friendly, especially the husband, who looked like the actor James Dean. Many of the neighbors began hanging out at their house while he fixed their cars, poured them drinks, and told a never-ending stream of jokes. His good nature made him a magnet for the kids in the neighborhood. I liked visiting my new neighbors because they treated me as a friend, not as a child. They had a way of making me feel special.

That special feeling turned into something else that, as an eleven-year-old, I could not understand. One day this man got very angry with me while a bunch of us kids were playing volleyball with him. I had chosen to be on the team opposite his. He ignored me during the game, aiming the ball away from me, not looking at me. I made some excuse to stop playing and went home, confused and hurt. What had I done?

The next day I played outside with my other friends. When he saw me, he called me over. He apologized for his behavior and said he had acted that way because he was jealous. "Jealous of what?" I remember asking.

As best I can now recall, he said something on the order of, "I have feelings for you that I shouldn't have. But don't worry. I will keep them to myself. Please don't be mad at me. I won't ever be mean to you again. But you can't tell anyone about our conversation."

I believed his promise as I tended to believe all the adults in my life. However, he broke it quickly with another bout of jealousy and anger, followed by another apology. This one came with a confession.

"Jane, I can't help myself. I'm in love with you. I've never felt this way about anyone before, and it's making me crazy. You have me wrapped around your little finger."

Of course, I felt no such power. In fact, I did not know what to do with such a secret. So I waited until he was at work one day and told his wife what he had said to me. She called him and asked him to come home immediately. What happened next confused me all the more. With the three of us sitting in their living room together, he said, "Jane, you misunderstood me. Yes, I love you, but I love you like a daughter."

I felt idiotic and humiliated, and I apologized for creating such a scene. He walked me out the door. As soon as his wife was out of earshot, he whispered, "Why did you tell her? If she thinks I'm in love with you, she'll kill herself. And I could go to jail, you know."

I don't remember how I responded because I was so shaken. Within minutes I went from feeling like a stupid kid to feeling responsible for someone else's life. I also felt ashamed, believing I had done something to cause this situation.

In my fear and shame, I did not tell my parents. I thought they might not believe me, because it sounded so ridiculous that a grown man would be in love with a child. Then I worried that they might believe me, which could be even worse: he would go to jail, his wife would commit suicide, the scandal would be embarrassing for my family, and we would have to move from my parents' dream home and neighborhood. I could not see any way out of this terrifying mess.

I believed I was bad for making him feel this way about me. Even at the age of eleven, as an avid reader, I remember comparing myself to Hester Prynne of *The Scarlet Letter,* who was branded for being a "loose" woman by having to wear a scarlet *A* on her chest for the rest of her life. I felt like a scarlet woman. I became estranged from my family, stuck with my secret and my shame. I stopped going over to his house and cut off all communication with him and his wife. When my parents asked me what happened, I lied, which only increased my guilt and isolation.

After three years of avoiding him, he caught up with me one day while I was walking my dog. His entreaty went something like, "You can come back over, Jane. I can control my feelings, I promise. Just give me a chance to be your friend again. I've missed you terribly. I can't stand that you won't talk to me or even wave from across the street. My wife misses you too."

I missed her and the specialness I had felt with them at first. I also felt jealous that all the other kids were always at his house laughing and playing. Being in exile felt like punishment. I was excited at the possibility of a return to "normalcy" and being part of the neighborhood again.

At first, he was very kind and polite toward me. I started to relax, enjoying the attention. Then, after a few months, he had another bout of jealousy. Again I cut off the relationship. Another year went by where once again I felt isolated and penalized.

After the end of that year, he repeated his pattern by again pursuing me. This time I was fifteen years old, with all the hormones and insecurity befitting a teenage girl with a mouth full of braces. He told me I was beautiful and that no one could ever love me as much as he did. He said he would die if he couldn't at least talk to me. I believed he loved me, and I fell in love with him. The truth was that I had loved him all along but had no place to channel that love when I was younger. We began having what I then thought of as "an affair." Our secret trysts were exciting and intense, as were our feelings for each other. I didn't know that I could have such strong feelings about anyone, or that someone could feel so passionate about me.

Participating in this relationship required lying to my parents once again, and I felt enormously guilty. By the age of seventeen, I was depressed from living a double life that was taking its toll on all my relationships. I never consciously thought about taking my own life, but I did hope for some disease that would take me away. I managed to contract the perfect illness: mononucleosis. I was hospitalized for weeks. At one point, the glands in my throat swelled up such that I could barely swallow.

As my condition worsened, the doctors prepared to perform an emergency tracheotomy. With that news, something clicked inside of me. I did not want surgery. I did not really want to waste any more of my life. One doctor came in and suggested I drink black tea because the tannic acid might shrink the swelling and help me avoid surgery. It worked. With that, I decided it was time to get better and get out of town.

I enrolled at a university ninety miles away. But of course I took myself, my self-judgment, and my guilt with me. I no longer believed I was worthy and (as you know from Chapter Four) acted the role of the good girl and married someone I didn't love. After my divorce, I still continued to validate my unworthiness by choosing alcoholic or abusive men. Little did I know what my first step in getting out of this endurance hell would entail.

What FEAR Really Is

I should tell you that I did something many of us do when we are ready to heal. Years after my divorce, I unconsciously re-created the relationship with the married neighbor I had run from ten years earlier. Here are the similarities. Believe it or not, I didn't notice them until I was months into the relationship.

My former neighbor had dropped out of high school as a teenager after flunking English. About two months into my "new" relationship, my boyfriend told me that he had dropped out of high school after flunking English. This isn't even the punch line. Although he had lived in rural areas for much of his childhood, his family moved to San Francisco during his high school years. It turns out that he attended the same high school as my neighbor, and they dropped out within one year of each other.

The supposed coincidences didn't stop there. My neighbor had a black shaggy poodle and owned a vintage Cadillac, a van, and a motorcycle. My new boyfriend had a white shaggy poodle, a vintage Cadillac, a van, and a motorcycle. Of course, he was abusive in ways that were strikingly similar. But I was as dense as a jungle about these parallels for months.

I met this boyfriend in a personal growth workshop that changed my perspective on many things. One of my mentor's first lessons was about "FEAR." He said that fear could stand for two things. The first was Forget Everything And Run. I recognized this one, of course; I had run away from my past as best as I could. "The problem with this," he said, "is that the universe does not want you to miss out on healing. So it won't let you get very far from your lessons. You will just have to replay your life until you figure out what you need to learn." *Groundhog Day* had not yet been written when he offered this wisdom. I took it in and started to sense that I hadn't gotten very far away after all.

Then he told us what FEAR could stand for if we wanted to change our relationship to it. "When you embrace fear as False Evidence Appearing Real, you stop running from it and start using it as your ally. You let fear become one of your teachers and your lessons come more easily."

Once I gave up the idea that I had to keep running from myself, my self-judgment, and my fear, I was able to begin paying attention to how my mind, body, heart, and spirit were often at odds with each other. I noticed that my mind, with all its chatter of *you're too this, you're not enough that, you'll never have what you want, and you don't deserve it anyway,* almost always got more attention than the rest of me. So I shifted my focus. What did my spirit want, anyway?

I had learned to think in terms of what I didn't want. I knew I didn't want to feel abused by men. I didn't want to judge myself anymore. I didn't want to take my self-judgment out on my body again. I didn't want to feel stuck in a vicious cycle.

☾ Time In ☾

Are you more aware of what you *don't* want or what you *do* want? If you start focusing on what you want, is your mind blank at first? When you let your mind get quiet and pay attention to your spirit, you will begin to hear or see or feel what you *do* want.

From Fear to Choice

I had to learn to think in terms of what I *did* want. If I kept thinking just in terms of what I *didn't* want, I would be left with a bunch of empty space in my life. But visualizing what I wanted was so unfamiliar to me that I had to practice the skill for many years.

The first thing I wanted was to end my déjà vu relationship. By saying affirmations, I mustered the courage to break up with my boyfriend and question my self-judgment. Affirmations, as you may remember, are not wishes. They are statements of what we want *expressed in present time*, as though they are already true. I began affirming that "I now deserve a relationship with a man who is wonderful and loving." I must admit, even while I was formulating this one, I was thinking, *Yeah, right*. Here's a clue: the less we trust an affirmation, the more the affirmation is right on target for us. If we already believed the affirmation, we wouldn't need to remind ourselves of it. The thoughts we do not yet believe but are willing to believe are the most powerful in countering our self-judgment and limiting beliefs.

Within three months of practicing this affirmation faithfully, I met my future husband. He was like no other man I had known or thought I deserved. With his kindness and support, I have been able to confront and heal my old belief about being unworthy.

My attempts to run from my self-judgment and avoid fear actually held me in bondage to my fear and dampened my capacity to thrive. Once I allowed fear to be my teacher—remembering that it is False Evidence Appearing Real—fear's spell was broken. I no longer brand myself as a scarlet woman, unworthy because of my past. Instead of placing my attention on avoiding what I don't want, I am able to glimpse more of what my spirit values.

I am also more able to see my so-called affair with a complexity that eluded me back when fear made the world so black and white. Although we had a very strong bond, my married neighbor manipulated me as a young girl into thinking that secrets and lies were necessary. He used my insecurity to woo me at an age that defines his actions as molestation. So I was victimized. But by taking the time to free myself of fear, judgment, and limiting beliefs, I no longer feel like a victim. In fact, I can imagine the very real possibility that the man who molested me was sexually abused as a child himself, and I have compassion for that little boy I never knew. I can also let go of the old, narrow version of my story and acknowledge that although I was molested, this relationship was important and complex.

This new understanding has given me the opportunity to notice many precessional effects. By enduring fear and self-judgment for so long, I became isolated. Perhaps the greatest lesson for me has been that, when I began to speak up about my experience, I found instant support and wise healers to guide me. I have learned to appreciate the freedom that knowing, speaking, and living my truth brings to my spirit.

Just as a skydiver prepares for a jump by taking lessons that include packing a parachute correctly and learning how to land safely, so must we break the spell of fear by being properly equipped. We are not required to jump out of an airplane without a parachute! Speaking our truth in spite of fear includes finding supportive people who do not feed into our fears. These are the people who have also had courage, the ones who can cheerlead us, the ones who will not use our fears or mistakes against us.

⏰ Time In ⏰

Think of one situation where fear is holding you back.
What kind of support do you need to help you with your
courage? Imagine yourself having broken fear's spell.
What do you feel about yourself? How does
your life look and feel different?

Each day we can find new and old reasons to be fearful. If fear
comes up for you today, make it your ally. Here are some real things
you can do to break the spell of fear:

- Remember that fear is False Evidence Appearing Real.
- Think of the worst-case scenario, and see yourself living
  through it with dignity.
- Remind yourself of a time in the past when your fear was not
  realized, or when you courageously met your fear head on.
- Get support from others.
- Create an affirmation, such as "I am now courageous,"
  "I now create support for facing my fears," or "I now choose
  my spirit's values over my protective guardian's fears."
- Remember that, no matter what the momentary outcome of
  facing down your fear brings, your worth as a person is constant and never in question.

❀ ❀

Fear blocks; truth flows. Fear takes us out of balance; the deeper truth
within our spirit brings us back into balance. Every time we turn
around and stare fear in the face, every time we choose courage over
fear, we say no to endurance and a big yes to creating an extraordinary life.

Chapter Six

Unchain Your Heart

Free Your Feelings

We know truth not only by reason but also by the heart.

—*Blaise Pascal*

Glenn was an alcoholic who felt he was ready to quit drinking. After two DUIs and the loss of several jobs and a long-term relationship, he knew it was time to turn his life around. The first six months of sobriety went fairly well. To him, this indicated that the alcohol had been his only problem. Now that he was sober, he felt more self-respect and confidence.

However, in his seventh month of sobriety he started to get hives—itchy red spots that would bubble up on his skin at a moment's notice. His doctor referred him to both a dermatologist and an allergist. He was prescribed steroids and anti-anxiety medication. But the steroids made it hard for him to sleep and affected his mood, much as alcohol had done previously. Glenn didn't like the familiar drugged feeling, as he described it, and came to a session hoping to wean himself off both medications.

"I never had this problem while I was drinking. It drives me crazy. I feel like having a beer or two just to stop the itching. Instead, I take the meds and feel drugged. It's a Catch-22."

I could see that he was suffering. "Glenn, what tends to bring the hives on?"

"Any time I feel stress I get them."

"Well, *stress* is kind of a general term. Can you connect any specific emotions with the hives?"

"I don't know," he said miserably. "I've learned that I used alcohol to drown my feelings. Maybe I'm just not used to feeling emotions, so everything feels like stress."

"That's a good point. Maybe we could explore the feelings that have led to your outbreaks."

He began to keep a "hives journal." Whenever he felt the hives coming on, he wrote down what he was feeling. The rule was that he had to name the emotion, not just call it stress. By the time he returned for his next session, he told me with some excitement that he had identified a pattern.

"It looks like I start to break out in hives when I'm angry."

"Maybe you've always been uncomfortable with anger, and you covered it up with alcohol."

"Yeah, but why would I get hives now? I didn't have them *before* I started drinking."

"How old were you when you started abusing alcohol?"

"I was fourteen."

"Fourteen is pretty young, Glenn. You might not have registered your feelings in the same way back then. But think about it now: Do you remember feeling angry at the age of fourteen?"

Without hesitation, he replied, "How about all the time?" He then proceeded to tell me his story, which included a teacher picking on him and humiliating him in front of the entire class. He went to a private boarding school that was very strict, and he felt he had no recourse for his complaints. His teacher informed his parents that Glenn was a problem. It was his word against the teacher's, and the adults in his life believed the teacher. To calm down, he started drinking before class every day and again at night.

"Glenn, it sounds as though your anger has never had any place to go. You must have felt helpless on top of feeling angry." As I said this, his face flushed with color as the old emotions rose up.

In the safe setting of my office, he felt free to experience the old anger and humiliation that had been bubbling up through his skin, looking for a way out. He cursed his teacher and the headmaster for lying to his family and for emotionally abusing him. When I asked him what limiting belief he had formed from that experience, he had no trouble naming it: "You can't trust people," he said. "They'll just lie and hurt you to save their own ass." In addition to this thought, he had a damning one about himself: "My feelings were useless. Everyone ignored them. They just made me miserable."

Your Early-Warning System

After Glenn released the anger from his past, his outbreaks diminished in frequency. The way he worked with his hives also changed; he stopped the medication and now thought of his hives as an early-warning system. Whenever he got the tingly sensation that preceded an outbreak, he would take some breaths and check in with his feelings, the ones underlying the stress. He would say his affirmation: "I, Glenn, do not deserve to be humiliated for my anger. I now respect and honor all my feelings." Most of the time, as he allowed himself to feel his emotions, his hives would recede quickly and dramatically.

If we stuff our emotions, *we will still feel the symptoms*. Why? Because our spirit is trying to get our attention any way it can! Many years ago, when I was traveling frequently to give seminars, I began to consistently develop a fever as I drove from my home to the airport. Although for a while I refused to take notice of my underlying sadness about leaving my family and friends, my spirit called out to me through my body, making me literally homesick. Once I finally made a deal with myself to travel only to the places I could feel excited about and only once a month, I no longer developed illnesses as I traveled.

🕐 Time In 🕐

Do you have physical symptoms that you can correlate
with particular emotions? What fear, self-judgment, or limiting
belief has stopped you from paying attention to your feelings?
What affirmation can you create to calm your guardian and
begin to honor your emotions and your spirit?

We are amazing creatures in our creative capacity to manifest physically our emotional truth and spiritual values. If we have any doubt about this, we can be reminded of our tears, laughter, and even perspiration, which we are able to create spontaneously from our thoughts and feelings. If we mask our emotions, our body and spirit will still speak their truth to us.

Lessons from *The Wizard of Oz*

Our thoughts create our emotions. We have to think something first in order to feel it. However, if we attend to our thoughts only and leave out what our heart knows, we become like the Tin Woodsman from the *Wizard of Oz*, searching everywhere for the emotions inside us. We require no wizard to complete us; to feel alive and inspired, we just need to connect our heart with our mind.

Recently, a landmark Harvard study determined that although many people believe a nice piece of jewelry, a larger home, or more money will make them happy, this satisfaction doesn't last long. Not surprisingly, perhaps, the researchers found that what makes us happiest for the greatest duration is something money can't buy: friendship. If we take this conclusion to heart—that what will make us happiest in the long run is our connection to others—then we have to believe that our best decisions, the ones that help us thrive the most, require both an open heart and an open mind.

Hannah was a daring, take-charge woman who was willing to be proactive in finding her soul mate. She courageously put her profile and picture on an online dating service and followed up with the men who responded. Only half in jest, she likened her online experience to job interviewing. Before she ever met a man in person, they would exchange a number of e-mails to make sure that they shared interests and that there were no obvious red flags. "After all," she said, "why waste time meeting someone if it isn't going to work out?"

She would then ensure that they had two decent phone conversations before deciding if she would take the next step of meeting a man for coffee. What she discovered, however, was that by the time she actually met her date face-to-face, there was little spontaneity. Most of the questions had been asked and answered. The "interview" was over before the coffee was cold.

By the time she came to me, she was frustrated. "Why isn't this working? I've made a long, detailed list of my criteria for a relationship. I read the men's lists to see if I'm a potential match. But nothing is happening."

Hannah was discovering that her mind alone could not create a loving relationship. She was trying to protect herself from wasting time and making mistakes by turning the process of finding love into a completely logical and structured pursuit. We explored her fear, self-judgment, and limiting beliefs before brainstorming a new strategy.

"Hannah," I asked, "what are your fears about finding a loving relationship?"

She had quite a list. "I'm afraid I won't ever find anyone that's right for me. I'm afraid I'm too picky. I'm afraid I'm too strong-willed for most men. I'm afraid that by the time I do find someone, it will be too late to have children."

She had a lot of evidence for her self-judgment, beliefs, and fears. Women who are strong are often publicly criticized and privately shunned. Science supports the concern that women have a harder time getting pregnant as they get older. I empathized with her. I imagined that if I had not met my husband, I might be in her same situation, putting out my "dating resume" on every legitimate Website I could find.

But I knew that her negative thoughts and fears had to have come from someplace closer than a magazine report on fertility. They usually begin when we first form our ideas about life and relationship— in other words, as children.

When I asked her if these thoughts had ever entered her mind as a girl, she said, "You bet. When I was seven, my mother had a miscarriage. She was thirty-three and she blamed the miscarriage on her age. Now I'm thirty-one and afraid. Also, my mom stayed at home to raise me. My dad didn't think women who worked were 'real women.'

He would say that men didn't like women who weren't feminine enough. I set out to prove him wrong. I went to college, traveled, and made a great career for myself. I left myself time to find a relationship and start a family, I thought. I tried not to hurry."

Proving others wrong is a sign that their words and beliefs are not only in the back of our mind but may be a driving force in our decisions. Insistence on "doing it *my* way" may actually be a reaction to others' ways—a function of our guardian mind, not our spirit. When a parent tells a child not to touch a hot stove, but the child touches it anyway, this is the child trying to prove his or her free will—and getting burned in the process. I asked Hannah if she ever felt she had perhaps spent too much energy and time trying to prove them wrong instead of listening to her own heart.

"It's so hard for me to know," she said, trying to figure it out. "I don't know what my heart would say. I've never listened to it, I guess. All my decisions have been based on what I believed was logical thinking."

"Even if your reasoning were impeccable, Hannah, how can you love from your reasoning alone? I think you found out from your 'job interview' dates that you can't."

Fortunately for Hannah, her longing for true intimacy was stronger than her fear-based arguments for creating a loving relationship from a list of criteria. She was also a quick study, and she took our conversation to heart. First, she changed her strategy, eliminating half of the information from her online profile. Then she decided to read only the first paragraph of a potential date's profile. If she felt something, she would initiate a connection. Other than making sure her physical safety wasn't compromised, she would leave the rest to chance and mystery.

Right away, she started to have a lot more fun and enjoyed more interesting dates. She found that she liked the element of surprise, and that her heart and mind, working together, did just fine at deciding if a second date was worthwhile.

Bad Feelings: An Oxymoron

Once we begin to welcome our feelings, acknowledging them as a beacon of light pointing the way toward our spirit, we learn wisdom that only the heart can teach us. But if we judge our feelings by categorizing them as good or bad, we miss out on this wisdom. We will try to hide the bad feelings out of shame, only to have them leak out in unanticipated and often unacceptable ways. This simply reinforces our belief that some feelings are unacceptable, rather than recognizing that by rejecting these feelings we are destined to behave inappropriately.

In Courtroom Earth, feelings are the enemy. To keep us as far away from them as possible, our protective guardian tries to scare us off, accusing us of being a crybaby, touchy, or foolish. But in Classroom Earth, no one is ever convicted of having a wrong feeling! In the classroom, all feelings are respected and mined for their invaluable information. In the classroom, we become curious students of our feelings, not judge and jury bent on assigning guilt for them.

Repression to Depression: The Not-So-Yellow-Brick Road

If we are afraid of our feelings, we may trick ourselves by intellectually acknowledging them while refusing to actually *feel* them. Saying "I'm happy" or "I'm sad" and actually *feeling* happiness or sadness are two different experiences, with two very different outcomes. The longer we judge our feelings and then repress them, the better we get at it. (Competency, unfortunately, can work against us as well as in our favor.) Nor do we get to pick and choose which feelings we shove down. Shove one, shove them all.

Eventually, after habitually repressing our feelings, we find ourselves asking, "Is that all there is?" while feeling symptoms of anxiety, depression, and hopelessness—clear markers that we are in our prison of endurance.

Like the Tin Woodsman, we search far and wide to find the feelings that are now locked inside us. Many people come for coaching because they feel empty, disconnected in some way. They have a vague sense of missing out on the depth of feeling that others seem to experience, but they can't seem to find a place of passion within themselves. Usually, they are convinced that their genetic makeup must differ from that of "emotional types." They may come in feeling bored and dissatisfied with life, having played hide-and-seek with their emotions for so long.

This was Allen's experience. When I first met him, he told me that he felt as though life were passing him by. He knew intellectually that he loved his two sons, but he couldn't feel his feelings for them. I thought he might be afraid of some of his feelings and asked him which ones might be most discomfiting for him. His response was one shared by many people who are afraid of their emotions: "I'm afraid that if I ever start to cry, I'll never stop."

He grew up in an environment he described as macho. He had three older brothers and a father who ruled the roost. He remembered falling off his bike when he was five years old and when he started crying his father said, "You're not hurt that badly. Don't be such a sissy." Allen tried to ignore the pain and stuff his humiliation but couldn't stop crying. Finally, his mother drove him to the emergency room, where doctors discovered he had broken his arm. He felt vindicated, but his father never apologized for ignoring his pain and shaming him, and he continued to denigrate Allen for any show of softer emotions.

No wonder Allen's guardian self wanted him to play it safe by becoming an emotional zombie. But he was in a dilemma with his sons. Whenever the boys showed him affection with hugs and kisses, he froze. He didn't know how to show soft feelings without thinking of himself as weak. When the boys cried, he was afraid that if he let them know their feelings were OK, other boys would taunt them for behaving like sissies. He did not want to be like his father, but he also did not know how or what to change.

Allen came to realize that his fear for his children was based on *his* childhood, not theirs. He was living in the past even though he was trying hard to escape it. His protective guardian concluded long ago that tears and affection led to humiliation. In spite of himself, he was passing along this belief to his boys and giving them the impression that he didn't care. Now he was desperate to break out of this vicious cycle.

He started to heal his relationship with his sons by first healing the relationship he had with the little boy inside him. When I asked him to visualize himself as a child, he said, "I was very cute and sweet, a lot like my younger son. I was also curious and tender." With this picture in mind, he talked to his "little guy," as he called him, telling him he had every right to cry and he didn't deserve to be humiliated for any of his feelings. This soliloquy marked the beginning of a new relationship for Allen, one that proved to be immensely helpful for him as a father. He found that how he talked to himself was just how he wished his father had spoken to him and how he was now willing to speak to his own sons.

Once he became accustomed to connecting with his little guy, he felt the desire to talk to his sons about his childhood experience of being scared to show his feelings. He wanted them to see him as he really was—sometimes strong, sometimes wise, sometimes vulnerable, but always real—just like them. He was surprised at their ability to take in such information at such a young age; he was touched by the compassion he saw in their little faces. He thought he might cry, being surrounded by their empathy, but still the old voices kept him from expressing his feelings fully.

Six months after he began telling his sons about his own childhood, the family dog died. Instead of keeping a stiff upper lip, Allen took the risk of crying in front of his children. At first they were so surprised that they just stared at him—they weren't used to emotions from their stoic dad. He told me later that he wanted to hide from the boys, but he faced down his fear and made himself stay in the room with them, asking them to hug and comfort him. After their initial shock wore off, his sons piled on top of him, squeezing him hard while they kissed his face and head. This made him cry all the more. Then his sons started crying too. Tenderly and sweetly, they took care of each other in their mutual grief. Allen had taken the courageous step of being vulnerable. He was rewarded with the discovery that his heart overflowed with love for his children. Life no longer passed him by. Each day now offered an opportunity to reclaim his heart and enjoy his family.

No More Censorship

If we were judged for our feelings as children and then learned to judge ourselves to keep control over our feelings, we may lose touch with our emotions and come to believe that they are unimportant. If that's what we decide, then we move dangerously close to believing that we ourselves are unimportant and therefore unworthy. Remember, this belief is not true, but it is a source of real suffering.

To honor ourselves and our emotions, we must stop censoring our feelings and offer ourselves compassion for all our emotions, including fear, shame, anger, and guilt. With compassion, we may discover more emotional nuances and layers than we suspected.

Allen discovered that underneath his humiliation he had always felt anger toward his dad for not paying attention to his real pain. Once he could identify why he always resented his father, who had died years earlier, he could let go of his guilt about it. With guilt no longer separating him from his other feelings, Allen was able to find some compassion for his father. He could imagine his father as a boy who must have been treated harshly for his feelings too.

Once we stop censoring our emotions, we find that the thought that they are our enemy is an illusion created by our fear (False Evidence Appearing Real). In truth, our emotions are a beacon, lighting the path toward our spirit. Since there are no successful detours to feelings anyway—since we cannot go around, under, or over our emotions without their sneaking back in—we may as well befriend them. Better yet, we can honor them.

Whenever Fred's teenage son Mike was running late for school in the morning, which was often, Fred would feel angry and lose his temper. He had told Mike that his tardiness meant Fred would arrive late to work and not get a parking place in the lot, which meant walking many long blocks to get to his office. In response, the boy promised to be more punctual, but their drama continued to replay itself. They both wanted coaching because the issue was damaging their relationship.

I started with Mike. "So, what's going on with you about getting ready for school in the morning?"

"I try to be ready, but I guess I just need to get up earlier." Mike seemed easygoing, but I wondered if this veneer was masking emotions held in check.

"How do you feel about your dad getting upset with you?" Mike just shrugged his shoulders in response.

When pressed for more, he continued. "I don't like my dad yelling at me, but I can't really blame him. I just wish he wasn't so uptight about work."

"What do you mean? What is he like about his work?"

"He spends all day there. Then he comes home and spends all night in his office working some more."

"Are you missing out on doing anything with your dad because he's been focused on work?"

Fred cut in. "The only thing I've missed out on is attending Mike's basketball tournaments. I had to miss three games because of meetings. I couldn't help it."

I turned to Fred. "Had you made an agreement with Mike that you would be there?"

"I don't know what I said. I think I said I'd try to make it, right, Mike?"

Now Mike let his anger show. "No, Dad, you didn't say you'd try. You said you'd be there. You said that all three times."

I intervened for a moment. "Mike, you feel your dad keeps breaking promises with you, right? So, do you feel obligated to keep your promises to him?"

"Hell no! If he can't make it to a game because he has to work all the time, why should I make it any easier for him? I don't owe him anything."

Fred was taken by surprise. "Mike, I didn't even know you were upset about me missing your games. When I asked you, you said it didn't matter."

"What was I supposed to say? You weren't going to come, so why would I make you feel worse about it?"

"Mike," I said, "by not telling your dad, you've turned your hurt into resentment. Does it seem possible that you're getting back at your dad by being late in the morning?"

"Whatever," he shrugged again. "But I'm not taking the blame for this. He doesn't keep his promises. I don't keep mine. He's supposed to be the role model, right?"

Now Fred was crushed. "I *am* supposed to be the role model, but I'm under a lot of deadline pressures at work. I try to keep my promises."

Although I had a lot of empathy for Fred's predicament, I knew that *trying* to keep promises was not going to feel the same to Mike as Fred's *keeping* them. Fred was setting his son up for hurt and disappointment. "You two are mirrors for each other. You both make agreements and you both fail to keep them, using excuses every time. If you continue to do this, your relationship will erode even more. You can only break the bond of trust so many times before it is permanently broken."

Fred was the first to respond. "I told myself that my broken promises weren't that big of a deal. I can see now that's not true. I'm sorry, Mike. Now that I realize how important it is to you that I come to the games when I say I will, I will be there no matter what. I promise."

Mike's stoicism finally ran out of steam. Mike pressed his fingers hard against his eyes to hold back all the hurt he had stuffed. "It's OK, Dad. I don't want you to come if you don't want to." Mike needed reassurance from his dad that he was important.

"I want to come, Mike. Maybe I didn't think I was that important to you anymore. We used to do a lot more together, but this year you started hanging out with your friends more. I just assumed my being around wasn't all that meaningful to you."

Mike couldn't talk anymore because he was overwhelmed with emotion. Fred didn't need to hear anything else from him anyway. Both of them understood that the issue was not punctuality. There were many emotions that needed to emerge and be honored for healing to occur. After hurt, resentment, anger, and shame were given their due, father and son could find the love and intimacy they had both feared were gone forever.

By working with their fear, hurt, and resentment, Fred and Mike uncovered their mutual limiting belief that they were not important to one another. Their emotions also softened them in a way that an intellectual dialogue could not have. By the end of the session, both father and son felt the compassion that often replaces anger once feelings are no longer censored.

Dignity, Not Denigration

We feel what we feel. When we stop hiding and defending our emotions, we no longer give them the power to shame us. They then have the power to illuminate our fears, thoughts, and perceptions.

The world always mirrors back to us our beliefs about ourselves. If we humiliate ourselves for our emotions and then censor or defend them, we subject ourselves to humiliation or disrespect from others. Mike and Fred, Allen and his sons, you and I deserve to honor our feelings. Treating ourselves with dignity, we let others know that this is all that we will accept. Inviting our emotions as guests to our table, we become host to an extraordinary gathering.

🕐   Time In   🕐

What feelings do you avoid because you consider them bad, difficult, embarrassing, or frightening: anger? fear? shame? hurt? Pick one of these emotions to focus on for a moment. How do you behave when you stuff this feeling? If you were honoring this feeling, how would you behave?

Our behavior reflects our thoughts about our feelings. Once we learn to treat ourselves with dignity, our behaviors demonstrate it. Instead of acting ashamed for feeling hurt, sad, or angry, now we hold our head up high, make direct eye contact, and express our emotions with genuine self-respect.

Beware of Boredom

Sheila smiled a lot, even while expressing boredom with her life. She had no real complaints, just a general malaise. Not even an upcoming vacation to Hawaii really excited her. She said she felt "flat" with friends, family, and work. I asked some general questions about her childhood to see where this might lead. As usual, her past held the key to her present.

"My father was a raging alcoholic. My mother walked out on him when I was seven."

I interrupted immediately. "What do you mean by 'walked out on him'? Did she take you with her?"

She answered without a trace of emotion, "No, I guess she walked out on me too. I never saw her again."

I let her continue, since mention of her mother's abandonment did not stir any feelings, at least not outwardly. She noted that she had worked for short stints at various jobs, leaving whenever she became bored, which didn't take very long. After telling me more about her boring existence, she suddenly looked at me with a gleam in her eye.

"There is one thing I do that no one knows about."

I took my cue and asked her what that was.

"I steal merchandise from department stores. But I'm not a kleptomaniac or anything. I don't keep the stuff. I give most of it away to friends or to Goodwill."

She went on to tell me that stealing gave her a thrill, and giving away the stolen goods made her feel "like Robin Hood."

When I suggested that she stole to alleviate her boredom and that she might have intense emotions underneath her boredom, she became angry. At least anger was better than that elusive Cheshire grin she had cultivated.

She missed her next appointment, without calling. Then I received an angry letter from her, telling me I had no right to assume anything about her and she should never have trusted me with her secret. I felt sad that Sheila was stopping just on the verge of what could be a real breakthrough for her, one that would put an end to her vicious cycle of boredom and thievery.

I was surprised when she called two years later for an appointment. We didn't discuss the letter because when she walked in grinless, with dark circles under eyes, we both knew we didn't need to.

"I was caught. They put me in jail. I was there for two days before my father, who had been drunk as usual so he didn't answer the phone, finally came and bailed me out. It was just a blouse. It wasn't even my size. I just thought it was pretty and that some poor woman who had nothing would really love it. Anyway, I got so mad at my dad that I just lost it with him."

"What did you say to him?"

"Leaving out the swear words, I told him that he was useless as a father and must have been even worse as a husband. I said that it was mostly his fault that I grew up without my mom, and that he was just a no-good drunk. I said a lot of things. Now that they're all out of me, I feel even worse. I thought I'd feel better."

"Maybe it's not all out of you. Maybe underneath the anger there's more. Are you ready this time to find out?"

"What have I got to lose?" was her response. Sometimes this is the best mental state to be in for healing. I asked her to breathe deeply for a few minutes because this can often help bring up emotions we are repressing. It didn't take long to surface her grief over being abandoned by her mother. She cried for a long, long time but discovered that her pain, like all our pain, was not really bottomless.

Sheila learned a lot about how her boredom served her well when she was too afraid to feel. But she had come to dread each day and certainly didn't want to go to jail again because of her boredom, which was confining enough. Like all of us, she had to find the courage to feel in order to heal.

 ### Process for Change
Feel to Heal

Do you ever find yourself holding your breath when you are anxious or fearful? The literal meaning of *inspire* is to breathe in. Most of us are in the habit of holding our breath or breathing in a shallow manner when we want to hold down an emotion; for some people, this even leads to hyperventilating or feeling faint or panicky. Focusing on our breath and paying attention to our feelings requires some perseverance, especially if we are in the habit of masking or repressing our emotions. But in terms of feeling inspired, the reward for making this connection is priceless.

1. Sit in a quiet place and close your eyes.

2. Take some deep breaths, breathing in through your nose and out through your mouth. Let your breath out fully.

3. Check in with your body. Do you feel any tightness or pain? Where? Give the pain or tightness a name (fear, hurt, anger, resentment, sadness). If your body feels light and open, give that an emotional name as well (joy, love, happiness).

4. Take some more breaths, in through your nose and out through your mouth, as you repeat to yourself, "I feel _____," naming the emotion you are experiencing at the moment. Your emotions may change as you continue to breathe.

5. Check in with your heart. Do you feel any tightness or pain? Do you feel that your heart area is closed, or open? Is it dark, or filled with light? Give any sensation the name of an emotion.

Whatever emotions you feel and name, just allow them to be. If they change, let that be. Let yourself *be*.

Boredom can be a big clue that we are ignoring or avoiding something. If we ignore our feelings or needs, boredom or fatigue may set in. Have you noticed that when you are bored the clock seems to move ever so slowly? But when you are enjoying yourself or captivated by something, you are surprised at how time flies.

When we ignore ourselves, every day can become boring and exhausting. When this happens, we start building up resentments, blaming the world, our company, our boss, our coworkers, our partners, or our children for our unhappiness. This was Esther's story.

A successful attorney in a large law firm, she exuded an air of confidence. But she came to coaching feeling bored and resentful. Her boss had strongly suggested she get an "attitude adjustment" because her sarcasm and demeaning comments demoralized others around her.

When I asked her what she wanted from her coaching session, she grew annoyed. She asked me to please just focus on the task at hand.

"Which is?" I asked.

"Which is my attitude. Just help me tweak that and I'll get out of your hair."

"First of all, you're not in my hair. Second, I don't know how to tweak your attitude."

Her impatience and anger with me mounted. "What am I supposed to do then? This is what my boss wanted me to do. Just do something quick and easy. Don't you make suggestions like, I don't know, tell me to put some pictures of some islands with palm trees up in my office or get a dog or find a hobby?"

"Obviously, you don't need me to make those suggestions. You know them all. What I wonder is, what do you really, really want?"

"It doesn't matter what I want. This is my life. This is what I went to law school for. You don't just go to law school, bust your butt to get into a good firm, bust your butt even harder to make partner, and then say, 'Gee, now I think I'll paint seashells.'"

Ignoring her condescension, I persevered. "What made you decide to go to law school?" She answered that she had done it as a dare. No one in her family thought she was law school material—including her attorney father. Yet she had proudly graduated third in her class at Yale. After congratulating her, I asked her if she had ever liked practicing law.

"No one likes practicing law. You do it for the ego trip and for the perks."

"Is your ego satisfied with its 'trip'? And are the perks still motivating you?"

"I don't even care about having made partner. The ego trip stopped the moment I graduated. As far as the perks, I'd rather be living in a little, whitewashed villa in Spain."

Esther got an earful of her spirit's truth in that moment. I asked her the most obvious question next. "What's stopping you?"

Esther had a list of reasons for not leaving her law practice to go live in Spain. But even to her, there was a tinny quality to these weak arguments. Finally she said, "Maybe the only thing that stops me is fear and wanting to still prove something to my parents." Concerned about getting back to her job and counting her billable hours, she left the session abruptly.

For a while, I didn't know what had become of her. Six months later, I received an e-mail from Esther—from Spain. She wasn't in a villa, but she was living in an apartment in Madrid and interpreting English for the Spanish government. She saw her session with me like this: "I came in like a little girl holding my fingers in both ears, eyes closed, yelling *no no no no no* because I was afraid of what I would hear. But it was only myself I was drowning out. I will never stick my fingers in my ears again, I promise."

We all change and grow; therefore, so do our feelings, needs, and wants. At one time in her life, Esther was focused on satisfying her guardian self's needs, not her spirit's truth. Her need to prove to her parents that she was capable overrode her true longings until boredom depleted so much joy from her life that she was compelled to pay attention. For Esther's spirit, enough was finally enough.

🕐 Time In 🕐

With what or whom do you feel bored? How are you
saying *no no no* to yourself? If you started saying
yes yes yes, what would you do differently?

Boredom keeps us safe from risking the new and unknown, where
we may be rejected or fail. But boredom can lead to slow, spiritual
withering. If we make our fears more real than our dreams, the boredom of sameness will keep us sitting on the sidelines.

Once we stop drowning out our spirit's whispers, we notice that
the boredom lifts and we become a passionate player, not a bench
warmer. Like Phil in *Groundhog Day*, we become less concerned with
fearful outcomes—a boring pastime—and become more energized by
this moment-to-moment game called Life.

The Power of Thoughts and Feelings

Any disconnection between head and heart will manifest somehow,
whether as boredom, resentment, depression, addiction, or physical
pain. Repressing our emotions is damaging. We delude ourselves into
thinking we can avoid our feelings without consequences. But the
pain that never goes away is the pain that is never fully felt. The body
always presents its bill.

Process for Change
Proving the Power of Your Thoughts and Feelings

If you would like to discover just how sensitive you are to your own
thoughts and feelings, how your mind and body are intertwined, try
this simple experiment with a partner:

1. Place one of your arms out at shoulder level in front of you and
   close your eyes. Think of something you have accomplished in

which you take particular pride. Once you have something in mind, indicate with a nod for your partner to press down on your outstretched arm as you resist the pressure.

2. Now put that same arm back up at shoulder level in front of you and close your eyes once again. Think of a time where you let yourself or someone else down, an incident about which you still feel some shame. Once you have something in mind, nod for your partner to press down on your arm as you resist the pressure. Is there a difference in your ability to resist your partner's pressure?

3. Now put your arm back up at shoulder level in front of you and close your eyes once again. Go back to your thought of something you accomplished. Take your time to really recall the details of the situation, including how you felt about your-self. When you are ready, nod for your partner to press down on your arm as you resist the pressure.

This experiment is based on kinesiology. The theory is that our thoughts and feelings are stored in our body. Our positive thoughts and feelings give us physical strength, while our painful thoughts and feelings sap our energy, making us weaker; hence, you might experi-ence having lower resistance to someone pressing down on your arm as you feel shame.

The arm-strength test also works well with truth and lies. If you think of a time when you mustered your courage and told your truth, you may notice that you have more strength and energy than you do when thinking of a time you lied.

※ ※

The energy we have used trying to forget the painful past or avoid a fearful future would be much better spent honoring our emotions. To become grateful for our emotions—all of them, not just the ones we would pick and choose—is to become empowered. Some emo-tions are familiar and some unexpected, but all are gifts that inspire us to thrive. Breathe in. Be inspired!

Chapter Seven

Take Off Your Armor

Heal Your Anger and Resentment

If you are patient in one moment of anger, you will
escape a hundred days of sorrow.

—*Chinese proverb*

You call the phone company with a problem, but you have to go
through five menu options before you speak to a live human being,
only to be told you have reached the wrong department and are put
on hold for ten minutes, listening to music you didn't like when it
was first released twenty years ago—and then the person who answers your call needs all your personal information but doesn't seem
to know (or care) about your problem. If you're getting angry just
reading this, I understand perfectly.

My fuse is lit by everything from waiting in a long line at the grocery store while the customer at the head of the line searches every
pocket for exact change to seeing a parent hit a child. I get furious if I
perceive any kind of unfairness toward my daughter and become resentful when someone is late for a meeting with me and doesn't call.
I have cursed at drivers who don't signal before turning and at ones
who drive too slowly when I'm in a hurry. I am insulted if my husband
uses Dijon instead of yellow mustard on my sandwich. More about
that in a minute.

Does any of this sound familiar? Deep down, most of us believe
our anger controls us, and this makes us wary, if not afraid, of our
anger. In reaction to our fear, we may push the anger way inside and
simmer like a human pressure cooker, becoming increasingly edgy as
the pressure builds or depressed from all the effort of turning our
anger inward on ourselves. So long as we avoid or repress our anger,

we treat it as our enemy instead of using it as the personal alarm system it is designed to be. Once we understand the source of our anger, we can come to appreciate its services and use it skillfully and wisely.

The True Source of Your Anger

You may blame your anger on your personality, your controlling mother, your alcoholic father, your steamroller of a husband who never listens, your disrespectful kids, the way the world is going today, or the planetary alignments. . . . Nope. If we stop to think about it, our anger stems from a belief that the world should somehow be different from how it is in that moment, and that if it were different, we would not suffer. In this way our anger gives us valuable feedback, letting us know that something requires our attention.

When something is being done to us that constitutes mistreatment, anger motivates us to give others the message that they cannot violate our body or our spirit. Anger at mistreatment often inspires positive social change, as with the civil rights movement and the women's movement. If reality does not correspond to our ideals and our sense of justice, anger can be our strongest ally.

It's pretty clear to me why I get angry whenever I see a child being abused. My anger leads me into action, urging me to seek safety for this child. But why do I get upset if my husband puts Dijon instead of yellow mustard on my sandwich? Is this situation akin to the righteous indignation that drives me to intervene on behalf of a child? Here's the difference: in the case of the mustard, the Dijon takes on symbolic significance. My anger is triggered by the belief that the world (in this case my husband) should be different (he should know my taste in mustard), and if it were different, I wouldn't suffer (believing he must not really love me).

It may be hard to believe I can drum up anger about mustard, but mustard may be to me what someone remembering your birthday or your favorite flowers is to you. If my husband spreads Dijon on my bread, I must be unimportant—*doesn't he know by now that I like yellow mustard?!* Mustard represents all the other times I have felt hurt when someone didn't care enough to pay attention to my needs and wants, large or small.

Anger is often a secondary emotion that our guardian self uses to mask more vulnerable emotions such as hurt, humiliation, or fear. Because I have a self-judgment that my upset over mustard is petty, I try to ignore my hurt, which survives in a new form by morphing into anger at my husband's forgetfulness. But of course, there is a price to pay. Instead of using the mustard incident as an opportunity to heal my hurt or insecurity, my guardian self looks for *more* evidence that I am not important to my husband. So even though he has consistently spread yellow mustard on my sandwiches for years now, my protective guardian can still occasionally manufacture evidence to feel slighted by him.

Anger Is a Time Machine

Anger seems to flood us suddenly and spontaneously. But if we slow down our mental processes a bit, we realize that a thought floated through *just before* we felt the anger. The thought sounded something like, "This shouldn't be. I don't like this. This hurts or scares me." The thought is often unconsciously triggered by some earlier event that resembles this situation, without our even being aware of it. We often get angry because we time-jump.

Sheldon's unwitting time-jumping was interfering with his relationship with his six-year-old daughter, Elena. He told me that he often got angry with her stubbornness: "She gets defiant whenever I ask her to do something she doesn't want to do. She will just announce to me that she's not going to do it, turn her head away, and walk off. That makes me so mad! But then I yell at her, and that makes her cry, and she begs me to forgive her. Then I feel so bad for blowing up at her that I take her out for ice cream."

He rocked back and forth, clearly upset. Then he continued. "I feel terrible. I know this is a really bad way to do it, and I keep saying I won't let this happen again. But I do, and I have no idea what to do differently."

I wondered exactly what was triggering his anger. "How do you think Elena should behave when you ask her to do something?"

"I just want her to do what I ask when I ask it. I think kids, especially six-year-olds, should do what their parents say."

I have learned not to argue with anyone's parenting beliefs directly because it distracts us from the more valuable insights and lessons that our children tend to call to our attention. "What happens inside you when Elena defies you? What other thoughts and feelings do you have?"

"Other than feeling angry, I guess I'm insulted."

"So you take it personally when she refuses to do something you want her to do?"

"I guess so. It feels personal."

"Does Elena's behavior remind you of any other time in your life when you were treated dismissively?"

"No, not really."

I couldn't imagine anyone thinking he had never had the experience of being ignored in some way, but this question obviously didn't mean much to Sheldon. So I tried another. "Did you ever act defiantly yourself, maybe with your dad or mom?"

"All kids do, don't they? I remember telling my dad to go to hell one time when he told me to mow the lawn. I wanted to finish eating and watching a TV program. He insisted that I do the yard work right then and there. When I swore at him, he smacked me across the face and sent my sandwich flying."

"Did you mow the lawn then?"

"No way! Since I had already been hit, I had nothing to lose except my dignity if I obeyed him. I walked out of the house and went to a friend's place. And you know what? I never mowed that damn lawn again, and he never asked."

"So your defiance worked, right? You won. Is this what you're afraid of with Elena? Do you think that if you back off once she'll never do what you ask again and you will have lost control?"

"Absolutely. She's so much like me it's scary. We're both hardheaded."

"Do you realize that you're judging her because you're judging yourself? And you're in fear on top of it—fear that you will lose her respect and obedience, the way your dad lost yours."

When Sheldon could see that his anger had been connected to his own past more than to his daughter's immediate behavior, his blinders fell to the ground. "No wonder I want to take her to ice cream afterwards. I'm so afraid that she'll be mad at me, even though she still cries and begs for my forgiveness at her age, that I try to buy her love back, don't I?" He paused. "I guess I've been taking it too personally when she doesn't do what I tell her to do."

"Did you mean it personally when you refused to mow the lawn?"

"No, not really. I was just a sixteen-year-old boy who wanted to be my own man. My dad couldn't see that I needed to feel more independent. When he interrupted what I was doing and ordered me to mow the lawn, it made me feel like a little kid, and that wasn't who I was anymore." He stopped. "He took everything so personally. Just like me, I guess."

He could now question his limiting belief that Elena's strong will would eventually lead to a split between them. He needed to change a few behaviors so that he did not make himself right about this belief and inadvertently create a self-fulfilling prophecy.

Changing Self-Fulfilling Prophecies

We came up with a plan. Before he asked Elena to do something, he would first check in with her to see what she was doing at the time. Knowing she was strong-willed, like him, he would give her the wiggle room he wished his dad had given him, such as allowing her to clean up her room within a certain time limit instead of having to jump at his command. He would pay more attention to see if she was tired or cranky, or even having fun at the time he asked for something. He would also let her negotiate with him more about chores, a valuable skill for a child to learn and for a parent to support. He looked forward to saying enough is enough to his fear that fathers inevitably lose the respect of their children.

⏱ Time In ⏱

What triggers your anger consistently? Does this person
or situation remind you of something in your past? Slow
down your reaction time: What else do you feel besides
anger? What limiting belief is attached to your anger?

Looking for what triggers our anger increases the odds that we
will not continue to perpetrate on others what has been done to us
in our past.

When Patrick strode into my office, everything about him said,
"Don't mess with me." Tattooed up and down both arms with barbed
wire and daggers, he described himself as "quick on the trigger." I
didn't know if he meant this literally or figuratively. He came to see
me because his wife was pregnant and he was worried that once he
became a father he would be as abusive to his child as he already was
to his wife.

"After every fight, I promise her I won't yell like that at her again.
But I don't stop. In fact, it's gotten worse. Last week I hit her—more
than once. She told me to get my ass in here or she'd divorce me,
even if she is pregnant."

I asked him why he thought he got so angry.

"I don't know. It doesn't take much, that's for sure. I'm afraid it's
genetic. My dad was a real treat to be around when he was mad, and
that was most of the time. When I was a kid, I'd say to myself, 'I'm
never going to be like him,' but here I am. They say the apple doesn't
fall far from the tree. I guess I'm just one rotten apple."

His concern that his hair-trigger temperament was hereditary may
have had some merit, but I knew that many people who have grown
up with parents who raged find ways to channel their own anger safely
and productively. Patrick had tried to rid himself of his anger, but it
required more than just *not* being like his father.

I asked him, "What triggers your anger the most?"

"I don't like when my wife criticizes me. It just sets me off."

When he thought about it, he recognized that the criticisms that bothered him most were the ones he believed about himself.

"Patrick, we all hate to be judged for what we judge ourselves for. We don't want others to see in us what we don't like in ourselves because we think that if they see it they won't love us. If they don't love us, they'll probably abandon us."

"If you're telling me that you and I are the same, I don't think so. You don't look like you go around hitting someone at the drop of a hat."

"It's not because I don't want to sometimes. It's just that when I'm defensive, I start looking at what's going on underneath. I look for those painful memories that have led to self-judgment and limiting beliefs. They are the triggers for my defensiveness." I stopped. "Patrick, I want you to spend five minutes writing down your worst self-judgments."

At first he hesitated, not accustomed to admitting he judged himself. He was much more comfortable with being angry than with being vulnerable. But he had committed to his wife and unborn child that he would become a better man, so he picked up his pen and began writing. I told him when the five minutes ended, but he kept writing. "Not yet," he said. "I'm not done."

Fifteen minutes later, he looked up at me with sadness in his eyes. "I had no idea how much of this crap I had inside of me. I must be an awful person. I bet your list is a lot shorter than mine."

"My list is probably at least as long," I replied, smiling.

I asked Patrick to read his list to me because it was important for him not to feel alone and isolated with his self-judgments, something we all tend to feel when deep in our doo-doo. His self-judgments included some pretty harsh words: "stupid idiot," "bastard," "liar," "ignorant."

"And how do your self-judgments serve you?"

"I would think they'd make me want to be a better person."

"Do they?"

"I guess not, because I've just gotten worse over the years."

"Welcome to the way life really works. We all—you included—experience reality on the basis of our thoughts. If you continue to believe all those awful judgments, you'll continue to hate yourself. You'll invite others to experience you as a stupid, hateful bastard, and you'll go on allowing your anger to hurt everyone in your life. You can't heal your anger or your self-judgments if you're determined to stay attached to them."

"What do you mean, 'attached'? I'm not *attached* to these words. That's how I am. They're true."

"I know it's hard to see it, but we will make real anything we are attached to believing. You've made these judgments real, and you'll keep making them real as long as you believe them. But that's a choice. You could choose instead to see that your self-judgments were formed by a young boy who believed his father more than he believed himself. And you are still believing your father."

We talked about his childhood to find out where and why he had come to believe the self-judgments that made him react so strongly to criticism. But we always kept the focus on his choices. He could decide to be right, that he was indeed a no-good, angry bastard, or he could get out of Courtroom Earth and join the rest of us students in the classroom.

For some reason, the image really piqued this tough guy's interest. "What do you do in Classroom Earth?"

"You treat yourself with compassion. When you start judging yourself, instead of turning the judgment into a beating you stop and offer yourself compassion for having such a thought. You change your self-judgment into an affirmation. Because once you start treating yourself better, you start treating others better too."

He asked for an example of an affirmation. "Well, you already do them in a negative way," I smiled, "and you've been very effective in affirming a whole raft of negative beliefs. So now, instead of repeating to yourself that you are a mean and frightening jerk, just like your dad, how about saying, 'I, Patrick, am respectful of myself and others.'"

"Okay, I guess I can do that," Patrick agreed. "Can I borrow your pen?" After writing the affirmation on his hand so he could remember it, he asked, "Is that it?"

"Well, that would be enough for most people to start with. But in your case, you can do one more thing."

"What's that?"

"You can stop giving yourself more evidence that you are right about being like your dad. You don't have to try being different. You *are* different. So quit trying to be right about your apple-and-tree theory. It's just one more limiting belief that makes you react to criticism. Let yourself be wrong about that, and start looking for evidence of how you are different."

I was asking a lot of Patrick to be willing to be wrong about his judgments and limiting beliefs. We grow so accustomed to our beliefs that we confuse them with facts. But if we want to step out of the angry, critical, and defensive environment of Courtroom Earth and hang out with other students in Classroom Earth, we have to challenge our self-judgment.

It's All Done with Mirrors

Once he began giving himself compassion for his self-judgment, he could slow down his reaction to others' criticism. Who was the real Patrick—without the defensiveness, without the bullying attitude, without being in his father's shadow? By letting his anger be his early-warning device, he was freer to find out who he really was. What he discovered was what many macho-acting men find out: he was very sensitive—a softie at heart. His feelings were always near the surface, a realization about himself that previously scared him. As he became more familiar with his true nature, he allowed his wife to see his vulnerability. This softened her toward him. She told him she had berated him in the past because nothing else seemed to get to him. Once their daughter was born, they both made a commitment never to yell or show violence in front of their child. They found this agreement easier to keep as he shed more and more of his former armor.

Like Patrick, we feel the pain from others' slings and arrows whenever they mirror a judgment we have about ourselves. For example, if someone calls you "stupid" but you genuinely believe you are intelligent, you do not have much of a reaction. You might wonder if this person actually judges himself or herself as stupid and is projecting this onto you. However, if you believe you are stupid and you are called "stupid," you may lose your objectivity and instead feel hurt, humiliated, or angry. If you feel angry, you might get defensive or verbally attack the other person.

⏰ Time In ⏰

Think about a time when you became defensive from being criticized. What self-judgment was the criticism mirroring?

If we take in a criticism, it is because we are still in Courtroom Earth, judging ourselves. Exiting the courtroom is not only necessary but healthy. It is easy to open the door to Classroom Earth:

1. Pay attention to any anger or defensiveness.
2. Trace these feelings back to your underlying self-judgment.
3. Remember that these thoughts are real, but they are not true.
4. Replace them with affirmations and compassion for yourself.
5. Gather new evidence to support your affirmations.

We feel less angry and defensive once we discover more about ourselves within the safe haven of the classroom.

Resentments Are Like Rubber Duckies

Stomach tight and aching, head pounding, jaw clenched tight—resentment is anger dug in for the long haul, and it makes sure we know it's there. We may lie in bed at night, kicking ourselves for not having come up with the perfect retort to someone's insult or abuse. The next day we wake up with a feeling of anxiety or dread, knowing we face another day afraid of acting incompetently and mishandling our anger, afraid we will end up humiliated or rejected. Groundhog Day again.

Resentment, anger's closest cousin, is anger that simmers. As we stuff our anger and convert it into resentment, it eventually spills out like acid from a cracked battery. Our children, our partners, staff, store clerks, even total strangers all get burned with the drippings of our resentment. Road rage is a good example of simmering resentment released unpredictably.

Charles landed in jail one night for chasing another motorist at high speed on the freeway. By the time the highway patrol caught up with him and pulled him over, he was still enraged at the other motorist for having cut in front of him. Charles had been seeing me for a while, and we both knew that his road rage came from another source. But he did not know just how much he was stuffing until he had time to think in his jail cell.

He had been enduring his boss's personal humiliations of him for months and suppressing his anger for what seemed like a good reason: he was waiting for a buyout that would bring him a significant amount in stock options. I had no right to tell him to risk his pot of gold, but the price he was paying for his silence was clearly taking a toll. In addition to his explosive road rage and the humiliation of landing in jail, he developed high blood pressure. He made a valiant attempt to put up with his situation, but by enduring, he now faced severe consequences. Although only Charles could decide if, in the end, it was all worthwhile, we don't always see ahead of time the potential consequences of enduring resentment. Resentment, left unattended, often surprises us with its insidious but potent backlash.

Three months later, Charles was informed that the buyout was delayed. According to him, this was normal. However, after six more months of delay and further endurance, along with some more angry blowups at family members and colleagues, he decided enough was enough and resigned. A year later, he heard that the buyout had fallen through. Though he felt relieved that he hadn't made a mistake financially, he regretted having stayed in an abusive situation and becoming abusive himself.

Few of us know what to do with our resentment. We are taught from an early age that we *should* forgive and forget; for many of us, turning the other cheek is a moral or religious imperative. Yet when we try to forgive others or try to stop thinking about the wrongs inflicted upon us, we often feel like a guilty failure. Our resentment keeps bobbing to the surface like a bath toy. In an attempt to let go of the past, we push our resentment down. But like a tubful of rubber duckies, resentments are not designed to stay submerged.

As we have seen throughout this book, emotions themselves are not the problem. We feel what we feel. It is our struggle with emotions that becomes problematic.

What Lies Beneath Resentment

Resentment is often triggered by a situation that appears impossible to resolve. If we feel powerless, we can build up resentment that makes us physically ill or emotionally distant. Resentment can throw us right back into our prison of endurance, as it did for Nicole.

She was an independent professional. Along with her husband, Andre, she was quite content to forgo having children. So after seven years of marriage, when Andre asked her to consider having a child, she was quite surprised. They spent the next two years discussing the idea. Finally, realizing they could never move through their fears or imagine the unknown joys and realities of parenting by making a list of pros and cons, they decided to try to get pregnant.

She conceived immediately. She loved pregnancy and adored their daughter, Kaylie, from the moment she laid eyes on her. Andre loved Kaylie too, but he began pulling away from Nicole and the baby emotionally. He still went through the motions of being a partner and parent, but Nicole could tell that his heart was not in it.

Over the next three years, he began to "forget" things—nothing big like birthdays, but little things like calling to get a babysitter or picking up something from the grocery store. Nicole grew more and more resentful as he seemed increasingly distant. Just after their daughter's third birthday, Nicole's seething resentment exploded into anger when he came home ten minutes later than he had promised.

She knew she wasn't angry about this incident as much as she was tired of tolerating a relationship that had come to feel artificial. She told him that she wanted to separate, even though the decision was both painful and frightening to her. She had never imagined her family breaking up, or raising their daughter separately; she didn't know how she would get along financially. She just knew she could no longer stand feeling resentful all the time.

The threat of separation served as a wake-up call for Andre. He admitted for the first time that, after Kaylie's birth, he became frightened. He saw Nicole as the better, more competent parent. When the baby seemed to prefer Nicole to him, he had his evidence. He felt like a satellite orbiting around the family, not a part of the solar system itself. To avoid his fears and pain, he fantasized about having affairs and even went so far as flirting and exchanging numbers with a woman.

Once Nicole voiced her decision to separate, he knew with certainty that he did not want these fantasies. He wanted to heal his fears and wounds and reconnect with Nicole and Kaylie. He begged his wife for another chance to prove that his commitment was real and permanent.

She felt betrayed and could not imagine trusting him again, but she was willing to give the relationship another try because so much was at stake. For the next six months, Andre consistently kept his word. He went to counseling to work on his fears, self-judgment, and limiting beliefs. He became affectionate and thoughtful with his wife and attentive to their daughter. Everything should have been fine. But Nicole was still enduring, locked in resentment. She judged herself for it because she felt he deserved more forgiveness than she was feeling.

Nicole's predicament is not unusual. We can feel stuck in resentment even though we think we should be able to forgive. The key to getting unstuck is to search underneath the resentment. Resentment, like anger, is not a primary emotion. It is a mix of emotions with one primary emotion at its core. That primary emotion is regret.

At first glance, Nicole seemed to have no reason for regret. She had done everything she could: she voiced her anger, set her boundaries, and got the result she wanted. But if we have resentment, we have regret along with it. As we begin to understand the connection between our resentments and our regrets, we get out of the prison of victimization that resentment keeps us locked in. Until she could uncover her regrets, she would continue to feel chained to her resentment.

How to Release Resentment

Somewhere, buried in her resentment, Nicole betrayed herself or broke an agreement with herself that she had not yet forgiven herself for. She began exploring her regrets by noticing her sadness: "I want to cry all the time for the missed opportunities during the first three years of Kaylie's life. We could have been loving partners instead of roommates with to-do lists. We could have enjoyed those first precious years together instead of wasting them in fear and resentment. I think I regret not confronting Andre sooner."

For too long, Nicole had played the role of the nag rather than face her fear of splitting apart her family. She couldn't know whether confronting her husband sooner would have worked. Maybe he would not have been ready to face his insecurity; he might have left instead. But because she so much wanted the perfect family picture, she had sacrificed being truthful for the façade of a life with Andre. This was her regret. To get out of victim consciousness, this was what she needed to forgive herself for.

Over time, as she practiced offering herself compassion and forgiveness, she felt relieved of the burden of resentment toward him, and they were able to reconnect with more intimacy and trust than ever before.

Process for Change
Healing Resentments

You *can* heal your resentments, and you can begin with a relationship you currently hold. If the person you feel resentment toward is willing to do this with you, both of you may find it powerful and freeing. Even if you do this process by yourself, releasing resentment will set you free.

1. Write down a resentment you hold toward someone.
2. What about this situation makes you feel sad?
3. How did you participate in co-creating this situation? What was your part in the dynamic?
4. What do you now regret about your participation?
5. Offer yourself forgiveness and compassion.

As you forgive yourself, you may find that you begin to feel forgiving toward the other person also. This is the nature of forgiveness.

Two examples demonstrate the power of this process. The first is Nicole's, and the second comes from another client's situation, one that touches on healing beliefs about unworthiness.

Example One

1. Write down a resentment you hold toward someone.

   I resent you for not being emotionally available to me or to our newborn daughter.

2. What is it about this situation that makes you feel sad?

   I feel so sad about not having the picture of family that I thought we were creating together. I miss the love and connection we had.

3. How did you participate in co-creating this situation? What was your part in the dynamic?

   I bit my tongue, stuffed my anger, and tried to nag you into opening your heart again. I endured feeling resentful for too long.

4. What do you now regret about your participation?

   I regret the lost time that we can never get back. I regret
   that I didn't have the courage to confront you sooner.
   I regret that I didn't trust myself or the universe enough to
   believe it could all work out no matter what you chose to do.

5. Offer yourself forgiveness and compassion.

   I am willing to forgive myself for not valuing my needs and
   intuition more, and for believing that I just had to endure.
   I offer myself compassion for the pain.

Example Two

1. Write down a resentment you hold toward someone.

   I resent you for buying a new car without telling me.

2. What is it about this situation that makes you feel sad?

   I would have liked to pick out a car together and have the
   excitement of this decision bond us more. I feel sad and hurt
   that you didn't want to include me.

3. How did you participate in co-creating this situation?
   What was your part in the dynamic?

   I have always been afraid to ask you to include me in major
   financial decisions since you earn more money than I do.

4. What do you now regret about your participation?

   I regret making money the issue. I regret devaluing myself
   by comparing our incomes. I regret not feeling like an equal
   partner with you and getting to enjoy the perks that go with
   feeling equal.

5. Offer yourself forgiveness and compassion.

   I am willing to forgive myself for not respecting myself or
   holding myself as an equal, regardless of my income. I offer
   myself compassion for the shame I took on needlessly.

Acknowledging that our resentments are fueled by our personal regrets, we free ourselves to step out of the victim role. It is not that we are letting others off the hook for unkind or unfair behavior; they are still responsible for their intention and action. We learn, however, that we remain stuck in resentment only as long as we hold onto the self-judgment and limiting beliefs that keep us enduring. The moment we uncover our regret, we recognize our own role in contributing to the dynamics that have fostered our resentment.

Resentment, like all our emotions, offers a hidden gift: it gives us the opportunity to pay attention to a self-judgment we have been ignoring, to change our relationship with others, and to become our own ally. As we acknowledge our regret, we move closer to forgiving ourselves for having endured rather than thrived.

※ ※

Enough is enough! Give yourself respect for *all* your feelings. By honoring your anger and resentment, by acknowledging feeling sad and blue, green with jealousy, red with anger, or golden with love, you break free from enduring a gray existence and find yourself in a richly hued world of feelings and experiences.

Chapter Eight

Give Yourself the Gift of Forgiveness

Live Compassionately

> Life is an adventure in forgiveness.
>
> —*Norman Cousins*

Lana was equipped with a quick, sharp-tongued wit. She described her ex-husband, Keith, as "the bastard in sheep's clothing" to anyone who would listen, telling stories about his past behavior with biting humor. The way Lana told it, her ex-husband had no redeeming qualities. He was barely human.

Pretty soon, I noticed that Lana wore the white hat in all of her stories. "Lana, you always come out smelling like a rose. Do other people think you're always so good?" I asked.

"Well, I'm sure my ex would tell a different story. And, no, I guess I'm not always the perfect friend either."

"Then tell me a little about your marriage from Keith's point of view."

Lana's wit was now a little more subdued. "I guess he would say I was angry, that I pushed his love away—an unforgiving woman."

"Is there truth to this?"

"Yes, but I wasn't going to let him get the better of me."

"So, Lana, how did your marriage get to be so contentious?"

At first, she seemed overwhelmed by the question. Then she responded with what seemed to her perfect logic. "Well, we fought a lot and the arguments were ugly—lots of insults, name-calling. But it's not my fault." Her protective guardian was in firm control. "I didn't deserve it," she said quickly. "I just picked someone who was typical."

"Typical according to what standard?"

"Typical like my father, like my two brothers, like my uncles."

125

Lana began to tell me about their hurtful and humiliating behavior toward the females in her household. I asked how she was treated.

"Like dirt. They watched football while we—my mother, sister, and I—were expected to serve them food and do dishes. They'd get drunk in front of the TV and then start putting us and all women down. They made inappropriate sexual remarks and they objectified all women. They were disgusting, really."

"And what did you believe about yourself?"

At first she wanted to think she had not believed anything about herself from this experience. But upon reflection she came up with this: "Before now, I thought I just believed that men were jerks. But I guess I also believed that in some way men were better than women. It's crazy, but I thought that they must know something I don't if they are the ones who get to sit there and I am the one who has to serve them. It was like they had some secret that I couldn't decode."

I admired her insight. "Can you imagine how your self-judgment of being less worthy has affected your choice in men?"

"Well, then it *is* all my fault. I guess I'm the real jerk here." Her guardian self was in high gear, creating a new self-judgment to shield her from the sadness and grief of acknowledging the power her thoughts had on her life.

"Now you're reinforcing your unworthiness—that's not why we're here! Get out of Courtroom Earth and sit here with me in Classroom Earth. Instead of judging yourself, give yourself some compassion for your suffering."

She looked at me in bewilderment, completely taken aback. "Huh?"

As hard as forgiving others can be, forgiving ourselves is usually much harder. We judge ourselves harshly, feeling that we don't deserve forgiveness from others or for ourselves. We imagine that keeping ourselves on the hook this way makes us more vigilant so we won't make the same mistake again. Yet nothing could be less true, since once we convince ourselves of our unworthiness we are back in endurance jail.

Forgiving Is a Necessity, Not a Luxury

We tend to chastise ourselves relentlessly, even though many religions teach the value of self-forgiveness. For example, Jews honor the spirit's desire for atonement on Yom Kippur, the highest holy day of the year. This holiday is meant to offer the experience of being *at one* (atone) with the world and with oneself. Jews do not eat, drink, or distract themselves in any way on this day. Instead, they apologize and seek forgiveness from others and for themselves.

According to the Roman Catholic religion, when Jesus was in his agony on the cross he said, "Forgive them, Father; they know not what they do." Catholics repeat this statement as a reminder that humanity's trespasses originate from our limiting beliefs and self-judgment turned into unconscious, self-fulfilling prophecies. By being assured of God's forgiveness, Catholics are asked to hold the same level of compassion for themselves and all others.

In Courtroom Earth, no one is allowed to make a mistake. When we do, we are severely punished—especially by ourselves. In Classroom Earth, it's a given that we all make mistakes sometimes. Because we know that mistakes are necessary for learning, we accept forgiveness from others and stop withholding it from ourselves.

The Fog Lifts

I asked Lana to take the first step in forgiving herself by making a list of all she needed to forgive herself for. We cannot forgive ourselves for what we are not yet acknowledging. So long as we are harsh with ourselves, mired in our self-judgment and limiting beliefs, we will resist compiling our list. We also continue to play the victim or the perpetrator in our relationships.

"I don't know how to do that," she said, her voice rising with tension. "And I'm afraid to. If I let down my guard, I'll never figure this out."

"The opposite is true, Lana. If you don't begin to forgive yourself and grieve your mistakes, you'll continue to punish yourself, either by picking another man like the men in your childhood or by isolating yourself out of fear."

"I've already isolated myself. I think my 'picker' is broken."

"Your 'picker' is your spirit, and it doesn't break. You just can't hear it through all your mind chatter."

She gave an enormous sigh and thoughtfully compiled her list. She discovered that she needed to forgive herself for believing that men knew something she didn't, for giving her power away to men, for thinking that no better relationship really existed, and for pushing away love. She also needed to forgive portraying herself as the victim and always making her husband out to be the bad guy.

By holding compassion in our heart, the fog lifts and we see more clearly. As she created her list, Lana began to reflect on her thoughts and behavior with less judgment. She was able to see why she had protected herself so thoroughly. She saw the nine-year-old girl having to serve beer and pretzels to disrespectful men. The girl felt trapped and resentful. Why wouldn't she decide that all men were jerks? This "wisdom" would protect her from them, she thought.

More important, she could now understand why she questioned her worth. No one in that house, male or female, gave her any reason to take pride in being female. All the women were subservient victims, at least in little Lana's eyes. With this new perspective, giving herself compassion became easier.

Recognizing Consequences

Now Lana was ready for the second step of the self-forgiveness process: to acknowledge the consequences of having wronged herself.

She could identify many consequences for holding onto her self-judgment and limiting beliefs: "I became cynical about love and intimacy early on, so I've never really had much love in my life. I attracted more of the same of what I was used to from my childhood, and wasted time and energy being right about men. I've created feeling lonely. I also hurt Keith. My distrust and cynicism couldn't have helped him be vulnerable with me."

Honoring Your Grief

Lana's tone had changed. There was a new sadness in her voice. This brought her to the third step of forgiveness, which is to grieve. Grief may often require weeks, months, or even years, and it may come in waves. The cause and effect of her endurance and suffering were hidden from Lana for a long, long time. Although she was able to feel sad about her choices, it would take her much longer to fully grieve the consequences of her self-judgment and limiting beliefs. I asked her to practice staying in the classroom by being careful not to go back to blaming and judging herself harshly, which is a way of avoiding grief.

The Road to a Clear Conscience

While dealing with her grief, Lana could simultaneously practice the fourth step, which is to make appropriate and openhearted amends.

She was not sure how to do this. "Who do I give amends to?"

"Whom have you wronged?"

"I've wronged myself mostly, from what I can see now. But I've also wronged Keith by making him out to be a monster."

"OK. It doesn't matter where you start. You can start with yourself, or you can begin by making amends to Keith."

"I think I would have an easier time forgiving myself if I apologized to him first."

Lana thus stumbled upon a key point: we may find it easier to forgive ourselves after we have cleared our conscience about what we have done to others. This is fine as long as we don't let others' forgiveness be a condition for forgiving ourselves. Forgiving ourselves is ultimately our responsibility, as she was beginning to see. If we leave it up to others to forgive us first, we are giving ourselves the message that we are not worthy unless others find us so. This thought puts us back in endurance, and possibly resentment.

The key to making amends to others is to simultaneously make them to ourselves. We don't need to wait for others to forgive or approve of us. No one but ourselves can clear our conscience. Therefore, self-forgiveness is not an indulgence; through self-forgiveness, we make amends and new agreements and practice valuing ourselves.

Sometimes we don't get the response we want or expect when we make our amends. This was Lana's fear.

"What if he tells me to go to hell?"

In her ideal scenario, Keith would be grateful for her revelations and apology. But as Henry David Thoreau points out, "It takes two to speak the truth; one to speak, and another to hear."

"He may not respond the way you would like, but you are doing this to clear your own conscience and heal yourself. You can hope that your apology will be accepted by Keith, but you can't focus on getting his approval or appreciation. Maybe he's too angry or hurt. Or he may reject your apology because he still feels guilty and hasn't begun to forgive himself. Who knows? Maybe he'll need time to realize that the woman apologizing to him is not the same sharp-tongued woman he lived with for so many years."

"It's just so hard to imagine saying these things to him without hearing 'I forgive you' back."

"The fact that you don't know what to expect in return makes you that much more courageous, Lana. But where do you want to hang out: in Courtroom Earth, where you continue to judge yourself and Keith, or Classroom Earth, where you get to tell the truth about your errors and go on to the next interesting life lesson?"

Once she felt prepared to make amends to him without the need for him to approve or appreciate her, she gave him a call. "I told him that I was sorry that I had made him out to be the bad guy in our marriage. I also told him that I now realize that I hadn't expected anything else. I decided to say to him that I now realize I deserve to have a respectful relationship with a man. He was dead silent on the other end of the phone. I couldn't see him, of course, so I have no idea what his reaction was. All he said was 'Thanks.' I think he was shocked. Heck, I was shocked. I thought he'd say more, maybe use what I was saying against me. But I think he could tell that I wouldn't take it from him this time. Neither one of us knew what to say after that, so we just said goodbye. In an odd way, it was the most intimate conversation he and I ever had."

Self-forgiveness may be one of our most difficult tasks. As Shakespeare noted, "To err is human; to forgive divine." But as Franklin P. Adams opined, "To err is human; to forgive, infrequent." If it were only difficult to forgive others and not ourselves, we would not suffer nearly as much as we do. But it is the harshness we pile on ourselves that keeps us in endurance. We are obligated to forgive ourselves for any part we have played in being hurt, humiliated, or abused. Self-forgiveness is one of the keys to freedom and thriving.

⏰ Time In ⏰

What have you not yet forgiven yourself for?
How do you treat yourself when you think of this
situation? Make amends to yourself. What can you
do to clear your conscience? What affirmation
of self-forgiveness can you create?

Lana, now ready to forgive herself, came up with this affirmation: "I, Lana, now give myself compassion for believing I was less worthy as a woman and for attracting validation for this into my life." She chose to get out of her prison of endurance and let compassion and self-forgiveness open her heart.

Farewell to Survival Strategies

In Courtroom Earth, we focus on others' wrongs or our own misdeeds. But behind every misdeed or mistake is a survival strategy run amok, as we can see in Marion's situation.

Marion had a falling-out with her old and dear friend Corey and could barely stand the discomfort of being so angry and humiliated. She wanted to forgive Corey but could not seem to find her way. I asked how she felt wronged by her.

Marion was able to give me her answer quickly. "Corey played one of my voice mails to a mutual friend. I feel conspired against."

"What did you say in the message?" I was curious to hear what Marion's part in the dynamic might have been.

"I said some nasty things out of anger. I accused her of something that I knew wasn't right the moment after it came out of my mouth. I wrote her that I was sorry in an e-mail afterwards, but it was too late. She won't speak to me and she won't apologize for playing that tape for someone else."

"So, you want her to apologize, just as you were willing to apologize to her. That's fair. But are you willing to forgive yourself?"

"I'm too mad at her to focus on forgiving myself."

"If you wait for her to apologize to you first before you forgive yourself, you are giving her your power. That will just increase your resentment and give you more to regret. So let's focus on you for a moment. What's your self-judgment about leaving the voice mail message?"

"Jane, I've done this kind of thing before. I speak first and then think later."

"All the more reason to focus on yourself. How is responding too quickly a survival strategy for you?"

She perked up. "Now *that* I can answer. In my house, growing up, if you didn't get your points made by being faster and louder, you lost."

"So, that's a perfect place to start with compassion and self-forgiveness. Now you know that you've been beating yourself up for a strategy that helped you survive. The best way to let go of any survival strategy is to see it is just that—survival—and not a thriving strategy. We have to notice first before we can change the way we do things. We have to say goodbye to it with respect, like saying goodbye to an old friend. You can now say, 'Thanks, but I have a better idea.'"

She heard this. "I can see how this talk-first, think-later skill served me as a kid. And really, it did protect me for years. But it's not doing a great job in my personal relationships, is it?"

She sent me an e-mail a week later to tell me she had decided, after starting her self-forgiveness process, to tell Corey she understood herself better and was working on slowing down her reactions and discussing her feelings more appropriately. She also asked Corey to talk about her decision to share the voice mail with their mutual friend. Marion was graced to have a friend like Corey, who turned out to be willing to be equally vulnerable. Corey admitted to Marion that she had looked to the friend for support for her anger because she didn't always trust her own reactions.

Upon reflection, Marion could see that Corey often did not trust her own feelings. She asked Corey to come to her directly next time and told her that she would not blame or humiliate her for her feelings. Corey agreed and apologized for her betrayal.

Marion and Corey could easily have lost their relationship by staying stuck in righteous indignation and using their survival strategies to try to protect themselves. Instead, they had the courage to be vulnerable and truthful, and to seek forgiveness with each other and within themselves.

 ### Process for Change
Self-Forgiveness

Self-forgiveness helps you bid old survival strategies adieu. Forgiving yourself is possible if you practice these five steps:

1. Make a list of the wrongs you have done to others and to yourself. See them as the survival strategies they are.
2. Acknowledge the consequences of these strategies on yourself and on others.
3. Grieve for your losses and for your mistakes.
4. Make amends with yourself and others.
5. Create affirmations to replace the self-judgments that drove you to using survival strategies.

As an additional affirmation, I gave Marion a revelation about forgiveness from Gandhi: "The weak can never forgive. Forgiveness is the attribute of the strong." Although it takes great strength to forgive others, it takes even greater strength to forgive ourselves.

The Three Fingers Rule

The compassionate and forgiving heart is the wise heart. The wise heart is able to release the past through forgiveness. With this release, we no longer give away our power and dignity; we learn to honor ourselves and our humanity.

No matter how much we forgive ourselves, we will continue to make mistakes, continue to react in fear using survival strategies rather than respond from love and truth, defend a position rather than listen openly, and point a finger judging others while three fingers point back at ourselves. This is all the more reason to embrace self-forgiveness.

We are all worthy of our own compassion. We are all worthy of forgiving ourselves for the pain and suffering created from our self-judgment and limiting beliefs. We are all worthy of attending to our spirit and of being inspired to become our own role model of benevolence.

The Courage to Clean Up Your Past

Once you know the value of self-forgiveness, you become more eager to resolve past trespasses and regrets. But what's the right way to do this? To right your past wrongs, you must prepare yourself for every possible outcome, including an unforgiving response or no response in return. To apologize because it is the right thing to do, and not because others will necessarily forgive you, takes great courage.

Consider the most appropriate way to communicate your amends. Would the individual you have wronged appreciate discussing this in person, getting a phone call, or receiving a letter or e-mail? Do not let your fear drive the decision on your means of communicating your amends. Let your spirit guide you. Regardless of the outcome, make an agreement with yourself up front that you will remember to acknowledge your own courage and commitment.

Sometimes we are ready to apologize and even compensate someone for our past mistakes, but those we wronged may no longer be in our lives. They may have died, or moved away, or we may have lost contact with them over the years. Take heart: this does not stop us from making amends with others and with ourselves.

Even if you cannot speak to a person about a situation for which you hold guilt, shame, or remorse, you can still write a letter to that person—*even though you know she will not receive it*. Write about your remorse along with your new insights. Be careful not to make excuses ("I pushed you away because you tried to get too close"); a real insight would be, "I pushed you away because I was afraid of being close, and that wasn't a good choice."

Put this letter in an envelope with the person's name on it (no address, no stamp), and place it in a mailbox. Be willing to suspend any disbelief as you close the mailbox. Trust, just for a moment, that we are all connected by an invisible but real energy. The energy of your letter will reach its destination, even though the letter itself will not. Remember, you are suspending disbelief in order to heal your past and release yourself. Your intention counts more than you can know. You will feel profound results from this process immediately, in ways that you cannot predict in advance.

Now give yourself some compassion for your past immaturity, ignorance, fear, or intolerance. Promise yourself that you will remember what you learned from this mistake. Make amends to yourself for all the suffering you have put yourself through since that event.

Asking for Apologies

What if you are the one deserving an apology from someone? We may not receive it, but by acknowledging that we deserve it we are saying to ourselves that we are worthy. We cannot always rely on the injuring party to alleviate our pain for us, but we have the right to ask for heartfelt amends. If we do receive the great gift of an apology, our spirit's longing for truth and justice is validated. Even without this gift, we have given dignity to our own pain.

If you cannot ask for amends because the person is no longer in your life or because your intuition tells you that he would not offer it to you, you can still heal. You can imagine what he would say if he were more healed now than at the time he hurt you. Your spirit will appreciate hearing the words it deserves to hear, even if the words need to come from within you.

The Gift That Keeps On Giving

Don't pressure yourself to forgive others; give yourself as much time as you need to forgive someone. Forgiveness is not time-bound. Forgiving others is not really about them anyway. It is a gift to ourselves. We are the ones holding the burden of anger, resentment, and pain. We deserve to be released from this burden. If we approach forgiveness as a process instead of as a momentary feeling, we stop pressuring ourselves to be better people. We stop pulling ourselves back into resentment. By no longer judging any of our feelings, we become inspired to forgive rather than obligated to do so.

You may find that one dose of forgiveness does not always do the trick, especially if you are not receiving amends from the person. Through the years, I have had many opportunities to practice forgiving the man who molested me. Forgiveness has come in fits and starts, in stages, and at unexpected times.

I have often thought that I'd forgiven him completely, only to discover new resentment popping up years later. Maybe I will never completely forgive him. Maybe I haven't fully forgiven myself for lying and betraying those I loved. But I promise that I will pay attention to my resentments, search for my deeper regrets, and continue to offer myself the compassion that was missing when I was a teenager. As I do this, I find myself released from being a mere survivor; I am free to experience the fullness of my life now.

Who knows why our lives unfold the way they do? Whether I look at my past as destiny, karma, fate, or serendipity, I am at choice about how I experience it. I can feel victimized by it, or I can discover my invaluable lessons through forgiveness and compassion.

Had I not had the relationship with my married neighbor in a crucial developmental stage of my life, I might not have been drawn to the field of coaching and transformational healing. Had I not practiced deception, I don't know that I would be capable of feeling compassion for others' fear of telling the truth. These are the precessional effects of my past, and I embrace them.

All forgiveness begins and ends with ourselves. As Alexander Solzhenitsyn wrote in *The Gulag Archipelago*: "If only it were all so simple! If only there were evil people somewhere committing evil deeds, and it were necessary only to separate them from the rest of us and destroy them. But the line dividing good and evil cuts through the heart of every human being. And who is willing to destroy a piece of his own heart?" We have all been sinners, and we have all been heroes. Our greatest challenge is to acknowledge our errors in thinking and action, atone to others and ourselves for what we have done, and attend to our spirit. In this way we mend our heart.

❁ ❁

By holding back on forgiveness, afraid to let go of our anger or to take responsibility for our regrets, we endure. This is our suffering. This is our prison. *This is unnecessary.* Forgiveness allows us to release our self-judgment, our resentment, and our remorse. It stops us from living in the past and having to re-create it over and over. Forgiveness helps us hear our spirit, which speaks in a true, clear voice.

The spirit—your spirit—is pure compassion, and its very nature is forgiving (for giving). To forgive, particularly to forgive ourselves, is to open our heart in spite of it all.

Chapter Nine

Be Inspired

Knowing, Speaking, and Living Your Truth

We have to learn that we can trust the truth and
that the truth will lead to freedom.

—*Jack Kornfield*

"Noah's been avoiding me for weeks. I'm so mad. How dare he avoid me when I've been such a good friend to him! He just uses me when *he* needs something. I should have realized how insensitive and uncaring he is."

Lisa was fuming. She was feeling angry and hurt, and deep down she was worried that Noah was rejecting her. To mask this fear, she focused on her judgment of him instead of on her pain.

But focusing on her judgments did not ease the pain. In fact, the more she thought about how he was avoiding her, the angrier and more hurt she became. "That's it. I'm going to call him and let him know exactly what I think of him!"

I'd heard Lisa fly off the handle like this many times before. But this time, as she related her pain to me, she caught herself in the act. She was becoming conscious and competent.

"Oh God," she said, stopping dead in her tracks and laughing. "I can't just let it rip anymore, can I? That's my survival strategy. I never realized this was going to be so *hard!*" She had come to a deep truth. If we've learned to calm our guardian self and become receptive to our spirit, we can no longer let ourselves get away with speaking less than our most vulnerable truth.

Intention Shapes Reality

Both our guardian self and our spirit express thoughts, feelings, and intentions, but they speak in two very different voices. The guardian, as we have seen, wages a defensive battle, often spewing judgments, limiting beliefs, and accusations. Conversely, the voice of our spirit always speaks from our highest thoughts and intentions.

Our thoughts and intentions are everything, and the energy of our intention can be felt in the subtlest ways. Our words convey only a fraction of our communication; some social scientists estimate that 90 percent of our messages are conveyed through tone of voice, facial expression, body language, and the more intangible but very real energy of intention.

In his book *The Hidden Messages in Water* (Beyond Words Publishing, 2004) a Japanese researcher, Dr. Masaru Emoto, introduced the concept of *hado* (rhymes with *shadow*) to describe the vibrational energy of words and thoughts. Dr. Emoto wanted to test the power of intention objectively, so he used a powerful dark-field microscope to photograph newly formed crystals of frozen water samples. As he spoke various words to the water or wrote words and placed them in the water, the water "changed its expression." In response to words such as *thank you* or *love* given either verbally or in writing, the water would form crystals of exquisite beauty. When *I hate you* was offered to the water, crystals did not form at all.

Water makes up about two-thirds of our body; is it too much to extrapolate that our thoughts, intentions, and words affect us in a very real way? Do we really believe that sticks and stones will break our bones but names will never hurt us?

To hold the highest intentions, we must take time to imagine the highest good. We have spent most of our life using the survival strategy of imagining the worst-case scenario of a confrontation so we can avoid it. Now we need to embrace a win-win intention that challenges us to aim higher, by imagining the best-case scenario and working toward creating more trust and connection in our life.

Once we calm the guardian self, we can communicate with more integrity, compassion, clarity, vulnerability, and wisdom. We may still sometimes feel like a novice, ready to admit to being conscious of our incompetence. But as with all new skills worth learning, our commitment to competency encourages us to dust ourselves off after our occasional (or frequent) pratfalls.

Honest Versus Truthful Speech

Speaking truthfully is not synonymous with the oversold virtue of simply being honest. Being truthful never has as its intention being hurtful. Truth is a much more complex blend of honesty mixed with compassion and vulnerability.

Honesty requires no vulnerability, humility, introspection, or compassion. For example, if I say to someone, "I think you are a jerk," I may be brutally honest, but I am not expressing my truth because behind any judgment of someone else must be a judgment of myself. And beneath any self-judgment, some painful memory is being triggered.

Honesty without compassion and vulnerability tends to lead to high-intensity emotions, polarized positions, and frequent fights. This kind of brutal honesty can break the fragile bonds of intimacy and trust.

We have all experienced being on the receiving end of someone's honesty; we may have felt humiliated or hurt. Perhaps we have listened to someone preach to us about our flaws while telling us they are doing so for our own good. We think we should be open to hearing feedback because we are taught to value honesty. Yet this confusion between honesty and truth makes us want to shun it—and the person "sharing" it—rather than seek it.

⏱ Time In ⏱

Recall a time when someone told you what he honestly thought of you. Did these thoughts contain judgments of you? How did you feel about what was shared? What did you feel about yourself afterward?

It is easier to be honest than it is to be truthful. Becoming truthful requires the courage to go beneath judgment to our very vulnerable core.

The Foundation for Win-Win

Truthful speech requires self-reflection and sensitivity to timing. Because it always includes our most vulnerable emotions, truthful speech has as its intention the strengthening of trust, which lays the groundwork for a win-win interaction.

When one of my daughter's middle school teachers called the children *brats* one day, I wanted to get on the phone and call her a few names in return. Would that have been honest? Absolutely. Would calling her names have vented my anger? Yes. Would my complaint stop her from calling the children names again? Hopefully. But I would not be speaking truthfully.

Was I angry at my daughter's teacher just because of what she said to the kids, or was I triggered by something in my own past? In truth, my anger ran far deeper than I realized at the time. I once had a beloved teacher who accused me unfairly of starting a fight with another girl in the playground at lunch. In fact, the other girl had attacked me. But this girl not only scraped her nails down my face while I stood there in shock but then ran to this favorite teacher of mine, who was on yard duty, and lied about the incident to avoid getting into trouble.

This teacher, who was always kind and thoughtful and had nurtured my intellect, walked over to me, and without allowing me to speak, started scolding me. She told me that she was disappointed in me and that she would have thought I was a better person. Then she told me to sit on a bench during recess for a week. When I opened my mouth to defend myself, she told me she didn't want to hear one word from me. The girl with the fingernails stood behind her, smirking like the cat that swallowed the canary.

I never did stand up for myself with this teacher. Instead, I turned some of my anger inward, judging myself for having been foolish enough to ever like and trust her. The rest of my anger I reserved for her, punishing her feebly by never speaking to her again.

I formed a few limiting beliefs from this incident. One was that people in authority have all the power. Another belief was that, even though someone has been nice in the past he or she can't necessarily be trusted. A third belief was that there is no such thing as justice.

So when my daughter's teacher made a blanket statement judging all the children (my daughter included), all my anger, hurt, self-judgment, and limiting beliefs were triggered from a past situation with a teacher who once judged me unfairly.

We can justify having a short fuse; we can even take pride in letting it rip. How often have we told stories of how we let somebody have it who offended us in some way? It feels good to be righteous, doesn't it? The problem for most of us is that the high we get off a flare-up is short-lived. As Laurence J. Peter so cleverly says, "Speak when you are angry—and you will make the best speech you will ever regret." The damage done is reflected in our future interactions with this person, and we are left with a nagging sense that we could have done better. The awkwardness and hurt linger long past the angry moment.

By recognizing that my anger was being triggered by the past, I was able to meet my daughter's teacher with a more open mind and heart. In so doing, I learned that she was under tremendous pressure. Her grown son was serving in the army and was in constant danger, and her elderly father needed her care daily. These two stresses were affecting her coping skills. This did not excuse her choice of words with the children, but I did feel compassion and no longer saw her as the enemy. When I asked if I could help in some way, she began crying softly and telling me she felt ashamed of her behavior. Instead of a predetermined confrontation where I attacked and she defended, we found common ground.

⏱ Time In ⏱

When was the last time you confronted someone?
Did you approach with compassion and truth? or with
blame and judgment? How would you have changed
your approach, given your current insights?

Where the Real Power Is

Honesty may include both blame and excuses. However, blame and excuses never lead to win-win, and they are dangerous to our spirit because they convince us that we are helpless ("I can't go back to school because of my children." "I can't travel because I don't have enough money." "I can't change jobs because I don't know what else I can do." "I can't leave him because he controls the purse strings.").

There is a more empowering and truthful telling of the statements I've just listed: "I don't want to go back to school until my children are older." "I choose to use my money for purposes other than travel." "I am afraid of changing careers and need to explore the limiting beliefs that are generating my fears." "I have let my husband control the purse strings and want to take responsibility for my financial situation now so that I can make better decisions."

Here's what distinguishes honest speech from truthful speech: truthful speech empowers us because it contains no blame—no blame of God or the universe, others, or ourselves. Truthful speech does not contain excuses and justifications for feeling victimized.

No *Ifs* or *Buts*

Have you ever had someone say to you, "I'm sorry if you feel that way"? What did you feel when you heard it? No doubt you didn't feel much of an apology heading your way.

The sincerity of an apology is compromised if you say, "I'm sorry if/but . . ." Does this mean you are not sorry for the intention, which may have been hurtful, but only sorry if the other person reacts? This is not an apology. This is a disguised accusation. The real meaning of the statement is, *You're overreacting and are to blame for having any hurt feelings. I take no responsibility. And if you believe it's not my fault, you will still like/love me.* This turns "I'm sorry" into a bargaining chip instead of an openhearted expression of remorse.

If you make an apology that contains a qualifier such as *but* or *if,* then your intentions are not yet focused on win-win. We all know when an apology is heartfelt. A heartfelt apology is much easier to accept than a loaded, insincere one. To be committed to win-win means that if you owe someone an amend, you do not dishonor yourself and keep yourself enduring out of fear by withholding this.

⏰ Time In ⏰

Can you recall receiving an apology that did not feel sincere? How did you feel? Can you recall giving a qualified apology (I'm sorry but . . .)? What happened from there?

If we owe an apology and we offer it with no strings attached, we instantly become more trustworthy. No strings attached means no conditions placed on another person. No strings attached in any of our communication—no attachment to being right, to convincing another person to approve of us or stay with us, or to winning against someone—creates a climate of win-win, offering the best chance of healing and creating more intimacy.

Conversely, if you don't feel responsible for another person's hurt in any way, then don't apologize. A more truthful statement might be, "I can see that you're hurt. Let's talk more about this, because that was not my intention. How did you take what I said?"

Sincere, unqualified apologies require courage. Your unwillingness to take the easy way out has a greater chance of leading to win-win because you are being truthful and trustworthy.

Hold a Pity Party

As Lisa was learning through her session about Noah, speaking truth requires self-awareness and the vulnerable expression of our deepest thoughts and feelings. If we disregard or hide our feelings because we fear pain or vulnerability, we stay in the realm of judgment and (mis)perception. As Virginia Woolf wrote, "If you do not tell the truth about yourself, you cannot tell it about other people." To Lisa, it may sound true to say "I feel like Noah's avoiding me," but placing the words *I feel* in front of a judgment or perception does not transform it into a truth.

To qualify as truthful speech, our communication must include our actual feelings.

Fortunately, Lisa wanted to be empowered, not victimized, with Noah. She was aware that her perceptions and judgments of him must be covering up the deeper truth of her hurt. She was also wise enough to know that if she wanted him to honor her feelings, she had to do the same for herself.

Her first step was to give herself compassion in the form of a pity party—yes, a pity party, with one guest: herself. The purpose of a pity party is to open the spout of compassion fully. It starts with a good whine and ends with a gentle soothing of the spirit. Lisa allowed herself to feel very sorry for her pain. This is what she said to herself: "Of course you're angry, Lisa. The way Noah treated you isn't fair. But it isn't just Noah. This is reminding you of lots of painful times where you've felt rejected. No wonder you're being triggered here. It all makes sense."

She did not have to deny herself compassion even if she might not get it from him, and her pity party was a great gift as well as a saving grace. A pity party does not turn us into a victim; it helps us begin to move through our feelings, especially those that involve hurt. If she had let her anger, judgment, and perceptions rule, she would have undermined any possibility for reconciliation.

🕐   Time In   🕐

Are you considering letting someone know that you
are hurt or angry? Are you willing to give yourself
a pity party first? You can hit pillows, shout out
your anger, or be as pathetic as you feel.

Here's what Lisa actually chose to say to Noah: "I'm really hurt
that you didn't call me last week—you said you would. My perception is that you don't value me as much as I value you. This brings up
old pain for me that I don't want to confuse with what's happening
now. So, could you tell me the truth about why you didn't call me?"

Rather than sparking a confrontation, she was truthful. Perhaps
because he was not boxed into a corner where his only acceptable
response would be a defense or an apology, he chose to be truthful
in return. "Lisa, I was afraid to call you last week," he said, much to
her surprise. "I needed your support, but lately I've felt like it's always me asking you for help. You don't seem to need my support as
much or as often, and I was afraid you'd think I was using you."

The irony of his holding back out of fear was that he got what he
most feared: she felt used by him anyway. But she might never have
found out about his fear had she not voiced more than just her perceptions and judgments. She had no control over his responses or his
willingness to be truthful with her, but she invited his truth by telling
her own. This is the essence of win-win communication: no one else
has to lose for us to win.

The Invitation

If we are afraid, we become defensive, which creates the tendency
to work toward lose-lose. In lose-lose, we substitute honest but possibly denigrating speech for truthful speech. If we seek revenge because, like Lisa, we are afraid of rejection, we sabotage ourselves and
our dynamic with another person.

With win-win, the truth coming from our heart and spirit sounds vulnerable rather than righteous. By keeping an open mind that we may still need to discover even deeper truths, we stop ourselves from sounding high and mighty and we invite others to be more vulnerable with us.

We want our word choice to reflect our best intentions, so it's important to consider the language we use with each other. Do our words invite argument, or intimacy and clarity? Do they demonstrate openness, or the need to be right? Do our words express judgments or feelings? Are we disagreeing in the courtroom, or in the classroom?

With a win-win intention, we recognize the distinction between perception and the truth of our feelings. The left side of the list here contains examples of perceptions and judgments that keep us in a lose-lose mind-set. The right side expresses the truth of our feelings and thoughts, empowering us to engage in a win-win dynamic.

Perceptions and Judgments (Lose-Lose)	Feelings and Vulnerable Thoughts (Win-Win)
You are too intense.	I feel inadequate trying to meet your emotional needs.
You are an angry person.	I feel scared of your anger.
If you loved me, you would do this for me.	I am disappointed that you don't want to do this for me. I feel unloved.
Whatever.	I feel powerless. I'm afraid we will never see eye to eye.

Look at the left-hand column and imagine being on the receiving end of these statements. Can you see how perceptions and judgments lead to inevitable melodrama and a lose-lose confrontation?

It is the right-hand column that offers the potential of win-win. Win-win does not mean acting nice. Win-win means we have the highest intention of speaking our truth with respect and openness, and we ask others to do the same. None of us can be totally free of perception and judgment, but with a win-win attitude we will not mistake them for our feelings or deeper truths.

The beauty of the win-win approach for speaking truthfully is that we can use it even if we feel hurt, upset, or betrayed by someone's words, deeds, or lies. Censoring ourselves keeps us in endurance. We have a duty to stop censoring our feelings and stand up for ourselves when we feel wronged. In our fear, we may admonish ourselves to live and let live, get over it, or even let people off the hook with "It's just their way." All these excuses are coverups for when we feel incompetent, unsure of our ability to communicate effectively. But remember that to get to stage three, conscious and competent, we must have the courage and willingness to practice. Once we commit to becoming competent, we can no longer imagine discussing our thoughts and feelings without the principles of win-win guiding us.

We may have concern about communicating openly and truthfully, even if we don't doubt the win-win process itself. Getting to win-win with others when we are hurt or angry does require some cooperation. Others must also be willing to tell us their deeper truth, let go of defensiveness, and be vulnerable with us. Sometimes this is a lot to expect and may not happen.

Others don't always feel safe with us; they may fear being wrong and getting abandoned; or they may feel guilty and try to cover up the guilt with defensiveness or counteraccusation. They may be stuck in a prison of isolation that they can't find a way out of. What clues will help you know how far to take a conversation?

The best way to check how likely another person is to hear your concerns and respond in a win-win manner is to notice if a lose-lose stance is being demonstrated. Is the other person calling you names, insulting you, threatening you physically or emotionally, interrupting, walking away, or screaming? If you experience any of these responses, stop the discussion. You cannot get to win-win unilaterally. If you continue to try to clear the air with someone who is acting this way, you are likely to feel doubly victimized and abused.

Sometimes it is enough to point out what isn't working and people will hear it. If you can ask someone to look at his behavior and he is able to shift from lose-lose to win-win, you can continue.

If not, let go of the discussion for the moment because you don't deserve to endure feeling victimized. Each of us has a secret history full of unconscious decisions, fear, emotional wounds, self-judgment, and limiting beliefs. This history can be running the show at any time. If the person you are approaching were history-free, he would be able to respond well. If you were history-free, you might not have your emotions triggered from his words or behavior. But none of us is history-free, and it is sometimes difficult to know when (and which) one of us is time-jumping, living in the past or dreading the future.

If someone cannot practice win-win with you, you may feel rejected, sad, or angry. Remember: it takes courage to reach out and wisdom to honor yourself and your relationship by inviting win-win. This may have to be enough, at least for a while.

When we understand the essential value of aspiring toward mutual respect and truth, we realize that win-win is not determined by any particular outcome. It is a frame of mind (and heart), and the moment we commit to it, we promote integrity, peace, and intimacy.

❀ ❀

By expressing our highest thoughts and intentions, we are able to live a true life, not just an honest one. By striving for the highest good we cannot help but invite and inspire others to create with us a more extraordinary life.

Chapter Ten

Breaking Free

Create Your Extraordinary Life

Be the person your dog thinks you are.
—*Bumper sticker*

After Phil the weatherman finally stopped listening to his fears, he took the risk to become a better person, speak from his spirit, and tell Rita his true feelings—and he woke up to a new day. Our spirit values taking risks and demonstrating courage and commitment. In the past, we wasted time evaluating our worth according to the last good or bad outcome, but we can now choose to break free of limiting thoughts and be the person we admire: our extraordinary self. It really is a brand new day.

Dreaming a New Dream

My client Donald's experience is a vivid reminder of the truth of architect Frank Lloyd Wright's wise words: "The thing always happens that you really believe in; and the belief in a thing makes it happen." Donald, a powerful, ruddy-complexioned Irishman, seemed (at least to his friends) to be leading a very good life already. From working hard every day landscaping other people's gardens, he gained a reputation that allowed him to bypass the usual business concerns of marketing or advertising. For this he was grateful.

But the truth was that he was working on other people's gardens while longing to have one for himself. He lived in an urban apartment with just a small, untended yard. He had every excuse for not having his own garden: he was too busy with other people's gardens, he didn't want to landscape a place that he rented but didn't own, and he was too tired to do more landscaping after a full day of back-breaking work.

All his reasons for not having a garden seemed real, but despite his excuses he was dissatisfied. He longed to create a soul-soothing garden of earthy scents and beauty. His guardian voice told him to stop wanting more for himself, yet his spirit knew what it longed for. Consequently, none of his guardian's reasons could appease him entirely, and he found himself envying his clients and resenting them for seemingly taking for granted the privilege of having a lovely garden.

One day he decided that enough was enough. He began exploring the limiting beliefs that were keeping him in endurance and came up with a deep-rooted (excuse the pun) belief and self-judgment: "I've always thought that I would never have what other people have. To top it off, I've also believed that I shouldn't want what others have—that envy is a sin. I guess it's no wonder I can't seem to let myself enjoy having a garden!"

He saw clearly how these thoughts had created his current dilemma. He had done enough work on himself to know that it all came down to a choice between holding resentment and valuing his spirit. Fortunately, he chose his spirit. He created a simple affirmation: "I, Donald, deserve to enjoy the same gifts I give to others." He reinforced his affirmation in small ways at first, by treating himself to a new shirt when he bought his daughter an outfit and buying flowers for his own apartment as he sent roses to a hospitalized friend.

Remarkably, he began shifting out of his habitual endurance pattern, and within two years he founded a neighborhood community garden on some vacant land in the city. His personal plot within the garden was so breathtakingly beautiful that it became a destination spot for tourists.

To make room for his dreams to come true, he gently told his guardian voice to take a rest and called on his spirit's deeper truth and guidance. In doing so, he created magic, not just for himself but for others as well. He literally transformed something ordinary into something extraordinary—and it all began with a shift in his thinking.

Hero Worship

Donald found a way to manifest one of his dreams, but he's not all that different from anyone else. As Vaclav Havel—playwright, revolutionary, and later president of the Czech Republic—said, "Hope is a state of mind . . . [the] ability to work for something because it is good, not just because it stands a chance to succeed." Isn't this hopeful quality the common denominator of those we admire and hold up as extraordinary?

We may believe that our heroes possess something we do not: more eloquence, courage, dedication, or luck. We may believe that our lives are smaller and that our influence is not as widespread or important. Yet our heroes and heroines are not necessarily specially gifted.

Even Gandhi, whom most people think of as an extraordinary human being, wrote in detail about his struggles with truth in his daily life. He found it far easier to adhere to noble truths—the truths outside himself—than to work on the simple challenges that faced him day-to-day; problems with lust, food, and shame plagued him for years. Eventually, Gandhi realized that it was not enough for him to be inspired by noble causes and courageous role models. He came to believe that seeking deeper truth requires moment-by-moment awareness—that sometimes it is *more* difficult to speak and live our deeper truth in all the little ways when no lofty ideal calls to us.

Is Gandhi really that much different from us? If you believe so, this is the last limiting belief we need to address because it is the final barrier to creating an extraordinary life.

Those we label as extraordinary or heroic stand out for one reason: they are guided by their spirit. The truth is that we admire them because our spirit recognizes and resonates with their spirit.

Process for Change
Becoming Your Own Hero

1. Think of someone you admire greatly. This may be someone you know personally, someone in the news, a person from history, a spiritual guide, or even a fictional character from a movie or book.
2. What is it about this person that you admire?
3. Now find the part of you that is like this extraordinary person.
4. For one day, demonstrate the qualities you admire in them.

⏱ Time In ⏱

How did you feel incorporating and practicing the traits of the person you admire? What does this teach you about yourself? Are you willing to demonstrate these qualities each day?

Everyday Illuminations

We do not need extraordinary events to create extraordinary lives. We can use everyday experience and lessons to break free from endurance and become admirable. Since daily life offers so many opportunities to misperceive or be fearful, each moment is rich with potential revelation. Even though we think we have left the courtroom for good, we may still find ourselves back in judgment, not because we have forgotten our lessons but because there is always more within us to be illuminated. I learned this unforgettably a few years ago when my family and I went skiing for a weekend with two other families.

We rented a house, and it was understood that we would all chip in for meals and help with the kids, who were still just learning to ski. By the second day, both my husband and I were perturbed with Len, the father of one of the boys in our group. He sat around watching TV while we all cooked, cleaned, played with the children, and got them outfitted for the slopes. His wife worked twice as hard to make up for what I perceived as his laziness.

The morning of our departure, we woke up to discover that a foot of snow had fallen during the night. Every adult except Len packed up the suitcases and leftover food, trudged out in the cold, loaded the vehicles, and shoveled snow. My mind was full of judgments, like popping popcorn. The final straw came when I saw Len's wife struggle to put chains on the car tires while Len watched more TV. By the time my husband and I pulled out of the driveway, we were spilling out all our judgments of Len, feeling empathy for his neglected wife and concern about the lessons their son must be learning about responsibility. We were in fine form, righteous in our indignation and sure of our perceptions.

Three months later, we found out that Len had liver cancer. He and his wife had known this at the time of our trip together. But they had decided to wait to tell people because they wanted to enjoy what might be their last weekend away with their son before Len's disease took over. They had considered canceling the trip but did not want to disappoint their son or break their financial commitment to the rest of us.

Had I not been so stuck in my judgment, I might have thought during the weekend to ask Len if he didn't feel well. I don't know if he would have shared that he was dying from cancer, but he might have acknowledged that he felt ill.

This experience humbled me and continues to remind me of how—even though I strive to stay in the classroom and let others be there too—my judgments and perceptions can limit, distort, and blind me to deeper truths. It never occurred to me that Len was anything but lazy and taking advantage of the rest of us. Why was that my assumption? What were my judgments of him telling me about myself?

If I were truthful with myself, I would admit that I tend to be a people pleaser. I have believed that others might like me only to the degree I prove to be helpful. Instead of using my judgments to illuminate something within myself, I completely misperceived someone who was bravely facing pain to give his son joy and keep an agreement with mere acquaintances.

Life doesn't always hand us as clear or poignant a situation as this one, but even daily events can serve to help us notice a detour or dead end, take out our map, and find the high road once more.

Daily Tonic for an Extraordinary Life

Living our truth cannot be for some future goal or noble end; our commitment to releasing judgment and limiting beliefs, practicing positive affirmation, honoring our emotions, and striving for win-win is the daily tonic for breaking free of endurance. Try as we might, we cannot compartmentalize our lives. To live an extraordinary life is to allow our spirit's energy into every cell of our being and into our every thought and action. As Gandhi wrote, "One cannot do right in one department of life while still occupied in doing wrong in any other department. Life is an indivisible whole."

Here's what this means in everyday life:

- By telling the clerk at the grocery checkout counter that she has given us too much change, we make integrity matter more than money.

- If our teenager asks us about our history with sex or drugs and we do not sugarcoat our past, we are a living example that truth matters more than our fear about being judged by our child.

- When we hear gossip and don't pass it along, we value compassion more than our momentary desire to feel important.

- Admitting to being selfish or unkind, we demonstrate courage and overcome the urge to be right or save face.

- In telling people we love them, unsure of whether they will say it in return, we make intimacy matter more than our fear of rejection.

Every action based on knowing, speaking, and living our truth takes us into extraordinary territory. Should we fall asleep and allow our protective guardian to take the wheel, our tires will roll into the same old rut. As we languish in endurance jail or stand trial over and over again in Courtroom Earth, we miss out on all the gifts—all the precessional effects. It takes courage to stay awake; it takes commitment to be your extraordinary self.

Remember, your thoughts are so powerful that you can make water crystallize in a beautiful pattern. Your thoughts are so powerful that you can inspire others, bring joy to them, give them hope, and bathe them in your love.

Karen had just moved in with Charlie. She was nervous about the decision because it meant that she had to give up the lease to her apartment. But she was nervous for another reason: she knew from experience that he seemed to pull away from her whenever they became close. Her response to his withdrawal was always to walk away from the relationship, knowing that inevitably he would come running after her again. In a way, this was her proof that he loved her. But making the commitment to live together had given her a chance to reflect on whether this dynamic was worth continuing for the rest of her life.

Sure enough, after less than a month of living together, Charlie announced that he wasn't certain about his feelings for Karen. He expected her to react as she always had, by walking away. But this time, instead of reacting from hurt, she paused and listened deeply to her spirit. For the first time, she saw her relationship with him in a completely different way.

Karen realized that Charlie was afraid of being abandoned, and his strategy was to leave before being left. She did love him, but her choice was clear: leave and never return to the relationship, or follow her heart and stay—risking total humiliation—on the chance that truth and love would override his fears. But even as she was getting ready to talk to him, her protective guardian's voice protested loudly: "What are you doing? Maybe he really doesn't love you and wants you to go."

But she tried instead to listen to her spirit's quiet encouragement to stay. Fearful but determined, she sat Charlie down and told him,

"I'm not going anywhere. I'm not going to help you be right again so that you can abandon me before you think I will abandon you. I'm not going to play the game of pretending I don't care so that you'll run after me again and I'll feel loved. I'm living here now, so unless you change the locks, you're stuck with me. I am staying because I believe that you love me as much as I love you."

He was dumbfounded. She had changed the rules. He couldn't really *make* her leave because she had already rented out her place and he would feel too guilty leaving her homeless. Then the truth of her words suddenly penetrated: maybe he *had* created this dilemma for himself. How many times had they played *come closer, go away, come back?* Emboldened by her truthful assessment of their relationship, he took the opportunity to speak his own truth.

"Karen," he said, "you're right. I've been afraid, so I don't really know what I feel half the time. Maybe I do love you the way you think. I know I love you whenever I think I'm going to lose you. But when we get close, I start to feel annoyed with you."

In the past, her first response to his annoyance would have been bleeped from a PG-rated movie. But instead of letting those words come out of her mouth, she watched them pass through her mind and dissipate, unsaid. She held firm and continued allowing her spirit to dominate the conversation. "Then be annoyed, Charlie. I think I can handle your annoyance—for a little while, at least—as long as I remind myself that you're using annoyance as a way to try to protect yourself from being rejected."

He noticed a new feeling for her at this moment: he admired her. How could he push away someone who was so admirable? Charlie and Karen made it through their rocky beginning. Both of them overcame fear, not by avoiding it but by remembering what fear stands for and staring it down. Over time, he allowed her in closer, and she felt touched by his courage and vulnerability. They were willing to risk everything—rejection, abandonment, humiliation, being wrong—for love. For that, they were rewarded with the miracle of extraordinary love and companionship.

Process for Change
Seeing Your Life as Extraordinary

When you wake up tomorrow morning, ask the universe or God for a favor. Ask that you be shown evidence that your life is extraordinary, that it is purposeful, and that your unique spirit matters. Promise in return to notice the evidence you are given. Repeat this every day—even after you are convinced.

What Really Matters

The brain tumor gave me the opportunity to live in the present and practice remembering that life is a miracle. You see, when I woke up from surgery, the doctor told me that he couldn't actually take the entire tumor out. He fervently hoped that by cauterizing "the hell out of it," as he put it, it wouldn't grow back, but he couldn't be sure. When I asked him what I should do from here, his advice was, "Enjoy your life."

So that is my commitment: to enjoy my life, and to share everything I am learning on how to go about it. It has come down to asking myself the simplest questions every morning: "What is it going to be today, Jane? Courtroom Earth or Classroom Earth, fear or truth, Groundhog Day or the day after, endurance or freedom, ordinary or extraordinary?"

Our greatest challenge is not simply making choices but choosing what really matters to our spirit. Truth matters to our tender spirits—the truth of our values and the truth of who we really want to become. Our truth matters because wherever we do not yet feel free, wherever we are hiding from ourselves or others, we are enduring rather than thriving. Freedom from fear, freedom from being run by our past, requires courage that is granted by our wise and joyful spirit.

When my friend's eleven-year-old son came home from school and told her he had lied that day to one of his teachers, he was at the same fork in the road we all face. He told his teacher that he left his homework at home when he had actually not done it. If he had told the truth, he would have faced the possible consequence of an F grade.

Now he had a stomachache and didn't feel like playing. I was touched by how tender this child still was to the impact of a lie on his spirit. He knew his body was presenting its bill. He was aware of the price he was paying for his choice, and he understood he was in endurance. All he needed was his mother's support that the price he was paying for his lie was far greater than the ramifications of an F on a homework assignment. She later told me that when she advised him to tell the truth, he let out a sigh of relief. He was being encouraged to value truth over expediency, earning him his freedom.

We are obligated to seek and offer what we have learned here: that judgment is merely a mirror of what we are still needing to heal, that limiting beliefs imprison us, and that to get off the merry-go-round of pain, endurance, and hopelessness we need to listen closely and well to our spirit.

Commit to Yourself

Here's your challenge: be more of who you already are, and take the risk to become someone you admire.

For one week—that's only seven days of your life—commit to making your spirit's deeper truths the focus of every interaction. This entails going beyond honesty by sharing at the most vulnerable level. Committing to your deeper truths means asking for what you want even though you may risk rejection. This commitment means giving generously to yourself, including offering yourself compassion whenever you need it. If you thrive more during this week, if you feel more inspired and freer, if you are more compassionate in word and deed, then you are on your path to creating your extraordinary life.

⏰ Time In ⏰

Imagine how your spirit would like to express who you are
becoming. Unlock yourself from your prison of endurance.
Let go of your limiting beliefs from the past and your fears
of the future. Become your own extraordinary self.

The last words of the Buddha were, "Be a lamp unto yourself;
make of yourself a light." Not "carry a lantern"; *be the light*. Most people who have chosen to align themselves with their spirit make a surprising discovery: it's not all that hard, and it's actually something of
a relief. We've been longing to live this way for most of our lives, and
now we can. Our spirit has boundless energy and bottomless curiosity. It longs to strive for our values and aspirations. Our spirit admires
heroes, not because it feels inferior to them but because it recognizes
them as kindred spirits.

Making a Difference

As our spirit flourishes, we become more concerned about others
and the world at large. We notice others' pain and suffering; their
search for deeper truth, intimacy, and peace; their fears that we can
now empathize with more deeply. As our numbness dissolves, old
feelings of helplessness are replaced by a longing to reach out. We
open our hearts as never before. In our gratitude and empathy, our
spirit whispers, "How can I help?"

As committed individuals, we call upon ourselves to drop our
armor, speak truth with compassion, live in accordance with our spirit,
recognize when enough is enough, and create peace and connection.

My Wishes for You

We have heard our spirit calling to us. Together, we are choosing
our truth over our fears. We are allowing our values to matter.

Now begins the next chapter of your story, the one that bears no resemblance to yesterday or last year, the one that is fueled by your highest intentions and spirit's longings. This is what I wish for you: may you wake up each morning inspired to create a new day. May you feel free to go joyfully in the direction of your spirit's longings and dreams. May you make the most of your extraordinary life.

※ ※

Stand in front of a mirror and look yourself in the eye. Just for a moment, do not put on the blinders of self-judgment. Look at the hero in the mirror. See the one who has courage. See the brave explorer who is breaking free of endurance in this very moment. See your spirit shining through, and breathe with it.

The Hindu *Namaste* greeting acknowledges the extraordinary spirit in each of us. Read it to yourself now:

> *I honor the place in you in which the entire Universe*
> *dwells.*
> *I honor the place in you which is of love, of truth,*
> *of light, and of peace.*
> *When you are in that place in you, and I am in that*
> *place in me,*
> *We are one.*

Namaste! Welcome to the day after Groundhog Day.

Acknowledgments

This book would be collecting dust under my bed if not for my magnificent agent, Catherine Fowler of the Redwood Agency. You are simultaneously a consummate professional and the most comforting hand holder. My deepest gratitude for your tireless efforts to take the book to the next level.

My heartfelt thanks to Naomi Lucks, the idea genius–editor, who is capable of shuffling chapters and paragraphs such that ideas flow with "simple" elegance.

This book would not have been born without my first editor, Priscilla Stuckey. Before I knew what constituted a manuscript, I handed you nothing more than a bunch of notes, and you had the decency not to laugh at me. With great tact, you helped transform a lot of ideas into the first working manuscript. I don't know if any other editor would have bothered.

My sincere gratitude to Sheryl Fullerton, my editor at Jossey-Bass, who offered wise feedback with a gentleness that is not required but is very much appreciated.

Although writing is often a solitary pursuit, it takes a village to bring a book out into the world. My village includes my clients and seminar participants, whose extraordinary courage and tenacity I admire greatly and whose insights I cherish.

When one is fortunate to have such outstanding and wise teachers, it is almost impossible not to learn. I would like to acknowledge Brandon St. John (may you rest in peace, or perhaps stir things up in another realm) and Marilyn Atteberry for creating the series of workshops that first opened my eyes and my heart to see deeper truth and begin my spiritual path. My other teachers, to whom I give a deep bow, are Elizabeth Kwiker, Ram Dass, Jack Kornfield, and Gangaji. You have inspired every paragraph of this book as well as my work for so many years. Thank you for your courageous, selfless, and loving teachings.

I would also like to thank Book Passage Bookstore in Corte Madera, California, for connecting aspiring writers with world-renowned editors, writers, and agents. I would not have known the steps to take without the crucial feedback of my teachers, author Rose Offner, and agent Amy Rennert, who donated so much of their time. Thanks to Left Coast Writers for all their insightful workshops and encouragement.

I have a friend who so believed in me that she backed my work financially as well as helping with child care often. Patte McDowell, you are a gem and the guru of fun. Thank you for reading the manuscript and saying that it made you proud to be my friend. You will never know how much that inspired me to continue through the many rewrites. Thank you also to Kathleen Dughi and Sally Thomas for all your enthusiasm, encouragement, honest appraisal, and vision (and more help with child care).

I am blessed to have a husband and daughter who make our home the loving space it is: Thank you, Lester, for never complaining about all the time this book took to write, which was much longer than either of us anticipated when I began. Thank you for your faith in my abilities and your respect for my passions. Thank you for listening to me when I needed to have a pity party. Thank you as well for reading and editing more versions of this book than anyone should have been subjected to.

Zoe, you embody all that is truthful and wise. You are remarkable, and I am grateful for your unconditional love. Thank you for teaching me by example—through your art, humor, intellect, and love for all living beings—how to create an extraordinary life every day. I delight in you, love you infinitely, and am the luckiest mommy in the whole world.

About the Author

For over twenty years, *Jane Straus* has maintained a private practice coaching individuals, couples, and families using the principles found in *Enough Is Enough!* She also speaks to various groups, provides consulting services for companies trapped in negative cultural patterns, and conducts in-depth seminars for organizations and individuals from all walks of life.

Jane's extensive list of clients has included the National Geographic Society, Environmental Protection Agency, California Department of Health Services, and National Park Service; nonprofit organizations such as the Sacramento and San Francisco AIDS Foundations, Yolo County Battered Women's Shelter, Davis Free Clinic, and Friends of the River; plus numerous hospitals and law firms.

She has been featured in the *Sacramento Bee* newspaper for her groundbreaking work and appeared as a guest expert on the CBS nationally syndicated program *Can This Marriage Be Saved?* She is the recipient of the Outstanding Young Woman of America award.

In addition to *Enough Is Enough!*, Jane has written and self-published *The Blue Book of Grammar and Punctuation* (www.grammarbook.com). This reference guide and workbook—which is often purchased in bulk by executives who recognize that proper grammar is increasingly important in the marketplace—has won numerous awards, including recognition by the BBC.

Jane lives in northern California with her husband, daughter, and dog.

More Ways to Say, "Enough Is Enough!"

*Inspiring Personal and Professional Services
from the One and Only Jane Straus*

You've read *Enough Is Enough!* from cover to cover. Now what? Where do you go from here? We each have unique circumstances that may create a barrier to creating our extraordinary life. For some people, reading this book is only the beginning. That's why Jane Straus provides more personalized, intensive ways to help you unlock your own prison door of endurance and break free from the patterns that may be holding you back.

- *One-on-One Coaching.* Let Jane help you identify your negative self-judgments and beliefs, transform fear into compassion and healing, and break free joyfully into a life that is aligned with your spiritual values and inner truth. Whether in person or via phone, her life-changing coaching sessions can help you craft a life of inspiration and integrity.

- *Workshops and Seminars.* Come together with like-minded groups of people to explore Jane's Enough Is Enough! principles in depth, share problems and solutions, and learn new methods for saying no to the situations that keep you from living a rich, satisfying, and spiritually-sound life.

- *Corporate and Nonprofit Consulting.* Perhaps your company, department, or team is suffering from a culture that's locked into negative, fear-based patterns. (Yes, enduring is as incompatible with achieving professional success as it is with attaining personal fulfillment.) Jane can help you—as a group and as individuals—escape your destructive habits and attitudes and create a dynamic, positive workplace that sparks inspiration, happiness, and even profitability.

- *Keynote Presentations.* Jane is delighted to speak on the principles found in this book. Audiences of all types—corporate, civic, and educational—find her to be an engaging, inspirational, and humorous presenter.

For more information on these and other services offered by Jane Straus, visit www.stopenduring.com, or call 800-644–3222.